I HAD A
NICE
TIME

and other lies...

Also by The Betches

Nice Is Just a Place in France

The Betches

I HAD A NICE TIME

and other lies...

HOW TO FIND LOVE
& SH*T LIKE THAT

G̈
GALLERY BOOKS
New York   London   Toronto   Sydney   New Delhi

G

GALLERY BOOKS
An Imprint of Simon & Schuster, Inc.
1230 Avenue of the Americas
New York, NY 10020

Copyright © 2016 by Jordana Abraham and Aleen Kuperman

First Gallery Books hardcover edition April 2016

GALLERY BOOKS and colophon are registered trademarks
of Simon & Schuster, Inc.

For information about special discounts for bulk purchases,
please contact Simon & Schuster Special Sales at 1-866-506-1949
or business@simonandschuster.com.

The Simon & Schuster Speakers Bureau can bring authors to your
live event. For more information or to book an event, contact
the Simon & Schuster Speakers Bureau at 1-866-248-3049
or visit our website at www.simonspeakers.com.

Design by Davina Mock-Maniscalco

Manufactured in the United States of America

10   9   8   7   6   5   4   3   2   1

The Library of Congress Cataloging-in-Publication Data

Names: Betches (Group)
Title: I had a nice time and other lies—: how to find love & sh*t like that /
    The Betches.
Description: New York : Gallery Books, 2016
Identifiers: LCCN 2015038504
Subjects: LCSH: Interpersonal relations—Humor. Self-actualization
(Psychology) BISAC: HUMOR / Topic / Relationships. HUMOR / Form /
Anecdotes. SELF-HELP /Personal Growth / Success.
Classification: LCC HM1106.B476   2016
    DDC 302—dc23
LC record available at http://lccn.loc.gov/2015038504

ISBN 978-1-5011-2094-7
ISBN 978-1-5011-2095-4 (ebook)

To all the hot messes who struggle to find love.

*A continuing special thanks to our friends and families
who supplied us with their crazy stories,
without which this book would
never have been written.*

Contents

Introduction

O h hey weirdo who reads dating books. Just coming home from that guy's apartment, the guy you swore you were going to have "the talk" with two years ago? Watching *Orange Is the New Black* for the third consecutive Saturday night? Consistently looking at engagement rings on Pinterest even though you haven't had a steady boyfriend in a while? You've come to the right place, Katherine Heigl. While most dating books are for newly divorced housewives with no marketable skills and girls who eat their feelings, this one is different. We're not going to give you step-by-step instructions on how to successfully date and marry the man of your dreams or even give you anecdotal evidence of that one girl who gained forty pounds and her boyfriend still loved her anyway. (The only way that won't matter is if he's also fat and/or works for her rich father and has an eye on the corner office.) We're here to tell you all those "road maps to finding The One" are bullshit, and the only way to master the art of not dying alone is realizing that dying alone is no big deal when you're going into the white light alongside the greatest person you know: You.

Most dating books will make you feel like a hopeless nicegirl, her lifeless body destined to be found among her twenty-seven cats while Taylor Swift's "oldies but goodies" play on repeat. This book will betch slap you to reality, help you get your shit together, and remind you that the old Tay was lame as fuck.

Forgot What a Nicegirl Is?

"The nicegirl plays by the rules without ever questioning them. She's dull, lacks depth, allows people to walk all over her yet brings nothing to the table herself. If she disappeared, you wouldn't even notice. She's the girl who rarely colors outside the lines of her life, and even then only in baby pink. She's the kind of girl who uses a real bookmark. In other words, she's boring as fuck."

—The Betches

Contrary to popular belief, you're not born knowing how to date and you have a lot of shit to learn. Plus, we're not here to sugarcoat dating advice. Adding sugar to anything is going to seriously limit your dating prospects. So break out the Splenda, throw your cats out the window, and get in, loser; we're going to fix your fucked-up love life.

But first, one of life's major questions (besides the most

obvious: "Is butter a carb?"): Why even be in a relationship in the first place?

The answer to this question seems to be obvious (duh, how else are you going to fulfill your dreams of having an envy-inducing wedding, popping out gorgeous kids with ironic first names, and packing cute little gluten- and dairy-free lunches?) but it turns out it's more complicated than it initially appears. Why even have a boyfriend? Unless you're like extremely religious—in which case you're already offended by much of this book—you don't need to date to have sex. You don't need to date to have kids (hello, in vitro). And you definitely don't have to date to be reminded how amazing and beautiful you are. That's what your grandma is for.

> *"I think we can all agree that sleeping around is a great way to meet people."*
> —Chelsea Handler

Being in a relationship isn't always fun anyway. All of a sudden you have someone who wants to know where you are, what you're doing, and to whom you're sending Snapchats all the fucking time. It's like, why are you so obsessed with me? If you're with the right person, however, it can be super fun, and from a purely selfish standpoint at the very least you'll learn a lot about yourself with each new relationship you fuck up. You'll get to discover interesting new things about yourself like that you can be really bitchy when you're hungry and that you could never handle dating a guy with just a green Amex. He might as well pay with food stamps.

But finding that person isn't easy . . . and if it is easy, then you're probably in that relationship for the wrong reasons. If you're lonely, get a friend. If you want attention, go on *The Bachelor*. If you want to have sex, walk outside.

The only reason you should be in a relationship is because your boyfriend/fiancé/husband/lover adds something awesome to your life, not because he completes it. You're a betch, you have the privilege of your own company. You're a hot commodity and your time and, more important, your affection are valuable, so why would you let just anyone in? I mean, would Beyoncé date Kevin Federline? Exactly.

Dating Exercise

Ask yourself: Is he the Jay Z to your Beyoncé?

If no: Dump him

If yes: Keep him

If maybe: What kind of car does he drive?

"There's nothing worse than the girl who has never been single."
—The Betches

It's better to be alone than to be with someone who sucks. While having a boyfriend has its perks, so does being single. For instance, you can go out whenever you want. You can make out with whomever you want. And if it's been a long winter, you don't even have to shave your vag. Win, win, win.

> *"Better alone than badly accompanied."*
> —Candace Bushnell, *Sex and the City*

One is not better than the other. It's about where you are in your life and what's best for you in the moment. If you think that a relationship is the key to your happiness you're as delusional as Karen.

Who the Fuck Is Karen?

Karen is our extremely delusional friend. She doesn't live in reality. She constantly thinks guys are into her who are clearly not. She's terrible at reading signals, and her mom is the only person who believes that Karen has a boyfriend. Really, Karen's "boyfriend" is the guy she fucked three times who finally asked for her number. Don't be a Karen.

Could I BE more annoying?

KAREN

WHY SHOULD YOU LISTEN TO US?

If you're a smart betch, you've already read our first book and learned how to win at basically everything. You learned the pitfalls of being too nice, what friends are socially acceptable to chill with, and to never ever admit that you don't know shit about wine. But what about dating? Yes, we covered that, too, but a lot has changed. We've grown up and the rules are different. Suddenly, it's sort of okay to online date, and the thought of being kind and caring to a guy is starting to not disgust you.

The simple truth is that dating in college and dating when you're in the state of mind to fuck around is a very different ball game than dating in the real world. There comes a point in every young betch's life when she gets bored of her thrice-weekly clubbing excursions and shambling to work hungover every Thursday. She realizes that she might have to entertain the idea of settling down into a long-term relationship, if only because everything else seems boring as fuck and she's already been to Ibiza three times. If you haven't hit that point yet, you will eventually. Even Paris Hilton doesn't want to be known as "that old bitch in the club" forever. No one likes a washed-up party girl, so eventually you're going to need to learn how to master the art of a long-term, committed relationship.

> *"Much of my high-jinks have been drug-related. When you're under 30, whatever, but once you're past 40 it's just ugly."*
>
> —Courtney Love

Unlike our grandparents, who actually needed to be married in order to leave their parents' houses, the modern betch can have an entire fulfilling life alone and with her besties. We don't need to accept the first man who offers us a four-karat ring, because we have options. We can be anything we want to be. This often means we settle down later in the game.

"When are you getting married? Dating anyone lately? How's that boy you were talking to last year, you know, the one whose parents were lawyers? He was nice," your parents and grandparents might ask you to death. But don't listen to them. All your grandma is concerned about is being alive for your wedding and all your mom is doing is comparing you to her own situation. She was married by twenty-five, and your grandma has only ever slept with one man. They had different pressures then, and that's why they're applying the same pressure to you. Don't get mad at them, just be like *Yah dating a few guys! Have a date tonight actually. Will let you know how it goes!* Then hang up and resume your Thursday night binge of *Scandal* and weed.

For our parents' and grandparents' generation, the name of the game was dependence. Getting out of the house, finding a husband to take care of you, popping out six kids. It was like passing the torch from your parents to your partner as the person who became responsible for you. But now it's all about independence for women . . . which is fucking amazing, but admittedly sometimes stressful because of that extreme pressure you may receive from your family who know nothing, Jon Snow.

Okay, so I'll just like, settle down when I'm bored and I feel like it, you think, stupidly. False. Most people suck at relationships and if you're a real betch, you're probably one of them. Our independent lifestyles full of Chanel bags, bottomless brunches, and yacht weeks are amazing, but they often leave us ill prepared for the world of real-life dating. Catch-22: It's precisely because we have so much fun on our own that dating can be so hard.

A time comes in a betch's life when she's gone to her one-thousandth single-girls night out and sort of feels tired of it all. The long pregames, the cocaine hangovers, sex with the guy whom she would never actually date once she got to know him—it becomes a drag. At this point she might say, *Hey, I've been single for enough time. I think I'm ready to find the perfect boyfriend who I can marry someday! Oh yay I'm excited.* Thinking you can magically enter the perfect relationship as soon as you've decided it's time is simply wrong. Most betches are quick to admit that they're bad at things like snowboarding or making their beds, but when it comes to relationships everyone is under the delusional impression that they can figure it out the first time they try. Do you think your spin instructor mastered her tap back the first time she stepped on the bike? No. Exactly.

So how will this new adult relationship differ from your college routine of balancing three back-burner bros and a shady asshole bro more seamlessly than your homework assignments? Sadly, it's going to involve some actual effort on your part and some important realizations. Dating and sex after college when you're looking for somebody who has the

potential for marriage involve actual self-reflection and sacrifice. Vom, we know, but like, it's true.

We're here to teach you how to remain a powerful, confident, independent betch while finding love. We'll give you
the secrets to staying hot and desired through every stage of
your relationship, making sure your sex life doesn't go to shit,
and giving you the keys to let go of the awful guys you've en-
tertained in the past to make room for the pro of your
dreams. We've mastered the art of dating with the help of
asshole bros, extra-nice guys, awkward situations, and too
many vodka sodas, and we think we're going to make it out
alive. So now it's time to pass on our divine truths to you.

You write us hundreds of thousands of "Dear Betch" letters looking for the keys to coming out on top while getting
the most out of your "relationships" and lucky for you we've
compiled this plethora of dating knowledge into a nonpa-
thetic guide. You're welcome.

While reading this book, remember the cardinal rule of
betchdom: Don't take yourself or anyone around you that seriously. There are some real truth gems in here but read this
book however the fuck you want. Don't be a trying-too-hard
loser and highlight this shit or give it to your dud nicegirl
friend to outline and summarize. Dating, much like this
book, is supposed to be fun and light so have a laugh, bask in
our awesomeness, and don't you dare pick up any other dating book but this one. No one wants to date the girl whose
bookshelf is lined with *The Rules* and *Men Are from Mars,
Women Are from Venus*.

Sure you're going to fuck up our advice. A lot. We've

fucked it up, too. A lot. That's why we're so smart. We've been around the block and learned the hard way. And honestly, we're still learning. It's important to remember through all your shitty dates, vicious fights, and nasty breakups that at the end of the day, whoever locks you down is fucking incredibly lucky and all the shit you've been through to find him will be worth it. There is no one out there like you and you are amazing, so even if you have days/weeks/months where you're feeling discouraged or lonely (gross) make like Dory from that movie where she has Alzheimer's and just keep swimming.

It's Me, the Head Pro. 'Sup?

Hi there. If you've looked to the Betches for dating advice prior to the year 0 BIHANTAOL (that's Before *I Had a Nice Time and Other Lies,* obviously), then we know each other. Not like, biblically, though I guess anything is possible. I mean that I'm the Head Pro, the Betches' resident guy expert for all *what the fuck does this text even mean?* issues, and chances are if you've sought advice, your e-mail has come through my in-box. I give betches advice. *Solicited* advice, unlike that guy Corey in your hall freshman year, who—news flash—was just trying to fuck you.

As you read this book, you'll see me pop in and out with my perspective on common dating shit. How soon is too soon to make a reservation for two (or more, if you like to party) at the Bone Zone Cafe? What are some dealbreakers that will cause your love interest to throw himself from the nearest tall building, resigning you to a life of loneliness and puppy Instagrams?

We can do this, together, you and I.

HAVING A BOYFRIEND FOR THE SAKE OF HAVING A BOYFRIEND

Just don't do it. A lot of (sad) girls go to bed at night fantasizing how nice it would be to finally become the girlfriend of the guy she's been pining over since her sophomore year of college. But what these girls need to realize is that just because he is their crush, just because they lie there thinking *oh my god he's so cute I'm definitely in love,* he is only that. A fucking crush. This guy is an illusion, a hologram of your perfect boyfriend with the face and body of the guy you think would look good with you in couples pics on Instagram. You're not in love. You definitely don't know this bro well enough to "love him," and if you ever got together you would probably realize that he sucks.

Dreaming about having a boyfriend is pathetic because it assumes that you need a guy to make you happy. By no means are we advocating that you should stay single forever. We just mean that a man should complement you, not complete you. Once you realize that you don't need a boyfriend to make your life amazing, only then might you actually find a boyfriend.

"He'll come when you're not looking/least expect it," says everyone you ever spoke to about the hardships of being single whom you subsequently wanted to shoot in the eye. But the root of your anger for said people is because deep down you know it's true. Don't be thirsty for a boyfriend. Don't be the girl who wants to leave a perfectly fun pregame because you don't want to date any of the guys there. Don't be so transparently desperate. Everyone will smell the desperation and walk the other way. Including your friends.

The moment you realize that you don't need to be completed is the moment when you are open to finding someone with whom you can share your green juices, summer weekends, and HBO Sunday nights, otherwise known as your happiness.

Note we used the word "share." When you share something with someone it means you are confident and content enough with what you have to give a piece of it away. The same goes with your happiness in relationships. Let's put this a little bit less abstractly. Say your bestie asks to borrow a black crop top. You're like, *Yeah def, you'll look way hot in this one* (you, of course, look hotter, but no need to say it aloud). Next day she gives it back to you but is like, *I'm so sorryyyyy but it's stained. I tried everything. Don't hate me.* You look at it, you look at her, you look at your drawer full of other black crop tops, and say, *OMG don't worry! There's more where that came from! Love you, Betch.*

But now let's say a three-month relationship you're in turns to shit. A can't-be-salvaged type of situation. The guy hurt you and he's a dick for it, but do not cry yourself to sleep every night to a Nicholas Sparks movie marathon because this guy completed you and now you don't know what to do without him. Because you know you were complete before him, instead you say, *Fuck it and fuck him. It's NBD, there's more where that came from.* This guy is your black crop top that got stained. If you know there's always more where that came from, it'll be easy to brush off the ones that are defective and bad for your look.

Sure, you may find someone who you think is the perfect guy for you for forever, but there's no guarantee that will always be the case. People change, betches are a force and we're constantly evolving. I mean, when the concept of marriage was invented we

> "It is a love based on giving and receiving as well as having and sharing. And the love that they give and have is shared and received. And through this having and giving and sharing and receiving, we too can share and love and have . . . and receive."
> —Joey Tribbiani

were all going to die at like, forty-five years old. The average now is like, a hundred or something. That's an additional 16,500 fewer calories or like, 5 pounds extra fucking birthday cake. Talk about a way fatter commitment.

Ultimately, your goal should be to meet a guy with whom you can enjoy your respective lives. He should share your values because you need to make decisions together in the future, as well as your interests because you need someone with whom to go shopping for expensive French wine. Having a life partner means that you can no longer do whatever the fuck you want. You can't like, not tell that person what you were doing because that's lying. And you definitely can't be shady. This sort of sounds miserable, right? Well that's why you shouldn't just date anyone. You shouldn't just accept any guy as your boyfriend because you like, want a boyfriend that week. You should date someone for whom it's worth giving up those freedoms. Freedoms like getting drunk and making out with whomever at whichever bar, not having anyone nag you about something you don't care about (i.e., bills and wearing sunscreen and eating froyo for dinner five nights a week without judgment). When you have a boyfriend you want him to be someone you don't want to be shady with, someone whom you want to tell everything you did that day, someone for whom you consider wearing a midriff-covering top. You'll know you're in love when your boyfriend wants to know what you had for brunch with your besties and you also like, can't wait to tell him you ate next to nothing.

QUOTES ABOUT LOVE AND WHY THEY'RE BULLSHIT

Since like, forever, people have been writing, singing, texting, rapping, whatever, about love. But because there's such an expansive amount of "wisdom" about the topic, and because the opinions of annoying hopeless romantics have deeply infiltrated our society, there's like, a lot of fucking bullshit out there. As betches, we are known for cutting the shit, and that's why we're going to break down the most clichéd sayings about love right here.

"Absence makes the heart grow fonder." Does it? DOES IT? Or is the saying, "Out of sight, out of mind" more true? These are two completely opposite pieces of advice regarding love that are repeated everywhere you go. One says that the time spent away from a loved one makes you closer to them. The other says that the time spent away will make you eventually forget them. So like, which one fucking is it?

Actually, we decided to pay attention in this one class this one time and we learned that according to some studies, the latter is the answer. Longer periods of time spent away from a loved one will make the feeling of hurt and longing crumble away. This agrees nicely with its counterpart phrase, "Time heals all wounds." Of course, a few days away from your boyfriend might make you want him more, but if you're looking to get over someone you better unfollow the fuck out of him on Instagram.

"Love is blind." People love whomever they want. Straight, homosexual, asexual, the list goes on. Of course, in that way love is blind. But when I notice my boyfriend has been eating four-too-many Shake Shack burgers lately, that's definitely a reason to put my cute little pedicured foot down. No one is blind to the dad bod, not even love.

"Opposites attract." Like, they don't really. Okay, if you're a blonde and are really attracted to a brunet, maybe that's the case. But a boyfriend who shares the same values as you (family, money, and other serious shit) is probably a better choice than one who cares about stuff you find unimportant.

Your boyfriend may know everything there is to know about politics and you may know everything there is to know about the Kardashians, but you still have an appreciation for spending time with your families. The politics/pop culture differences don't make you opposites, they suggest you might have slightly different interests. But the fact that you both sincerely care about staying close with your siblings and want to spend money on traveling means that you technically are more similar than you are different.

Also, a lot of people tend to be attracted to people who share physical traits of theirs. This is probably a manifestation of a betch's true desire to date herself, which is sort of impossible, so she dates someone who looks like her. So really what's the correct answer? There isn't one. Love whom you want to love, and leave us the fuck alone.

"All is fair in love and war." You may have heard this one from *How to Lose a Guy in 10 Days*. Last time we checked it's not cool to waterboard your boyfriend for forgetting to ask for spicy mayo. Not the best example, but then again in war you can spy, kill, torture, or any of that other cray shit we saw in *Zero Dark Thirty*. That shit's not really applicable in love. You can't just do whatever you want, ruin as many people's lives just so long as you can make a name for yourself as an investigatory journalist for the sake of love. In other words, you can't just be an asshole because you're into someone.

"You Don't Know You're Beautiful, That's What Makes You Beautiful." Ummm, fairly certain my bimonthly eyebrow threading, eyelash extensions, and $100-a-tube bronzer help make me beautiful. Like, obviously we try to be humble about it, but if we're hot, and we know we're hot, Harry Styles would definitely be into it. Also, if you're walking around crying that you're not gorgeous but you look like Kendall Jenner, no one, I repeat no one will want you, you grotsky little biatch.

"All you need is love." Pretty sure we also need water, food, shelter, vodka, and Netflix.

"You Complete Me." Don't even. Just don't even.

CUE THE TEARS AND CHOCOLATE: THERE'S NO SUCH THING AS A SOUL MATE

Let go of the ridiculous notion of "The One." Do it, right now. Shut your eyes, picture the words "The One" and then crush them in your mind-vise. There's no such thing as a soul mate. Besides the fact that that term is as gag inducing as the thought of eating anything off the McDonald's dollar menu sober, the concept of soul mates always was, is now, and will always be bullshit. Why? Because there are over seven billion people in the world, and more than just one of them is right for you.

The right guy for you is the guy who wants what you want at the same time as you. That's called luck and some people get lucky a lot. Some people get lucky less often. Some people meet a person who's great for them when they're seventeen and live happily ever after or until they're so bored they want to shoot themselves in the face. Some people won't meet them until they're forty-five or eighty or never.

The one thing we're convinced of is that there are definitely people out there who are better suited for you than others. If you want to call these people "ones" you can, but the important thing to remember is that there isn't just one of them. The only reason the term "The One" exists is because the phrase "I've finally found the one of a dozen guys out there for me" somehow sounds less romantic.

> *"There is no such thing as a soul mate . . . and who would want there to be? I don't want half of a shared soul. I want my own damn soul."*
>
> —Rachel Cohn and David Levithan, some authors

The thing to remember is that it's not just about finding the person for you. It's about finding a person who's right for you at the exact same time that you are right for them. Some people will meet ten guys who are compatible with them and some will meet one or even none. Some women meet a guy who's super compatible for what she wants in the moment, but he couldn't be less ready for a relationship. Don't let this information discourage you. You wouldn't want there to be a perfect prince who completes you, because, like we said, you don't need completing. Plus, we just told you there's no such thing as one soul mate so your chances of finding someone just increased by like, a billion percent. Math, fucking duh.

By picking up this book you're one step closer to not taking dating so seriously and by doing so, cultivating your love of yourself and learning more about what makes you tick and who you are. That doesn't mean it's ever okay to pluck your chin in front of a guy, but it does mean that you can have a great time while growing in life, and that includes relationships.

Try to have fun and find someone who supports you. Sometimes you'll fuck that up, most people do. But who gives a shit? Happiness is not about your destination, it's about how on point your hair looks during the ride.

So get ready, Betches, we're about to drop some truth bombs onto your beautifully balayaged heads.

1

Hot Messes
Need Love Too

Preparing to Date

D ating isn't easy. If it were, you wouldn't be reading this book. Yes, betches are inherently amazing people who look like they have their shit together, but deep down every single one of us has issues. Depending on how serious those issues are, they typically are reflected by the way each person acts, especially when that person is trying to get to know someone in a romantic sense. Enter the first date.

Unless you're extremely rich, an Insta-celeb, a real celeb, or are a distant relative of the Hadid-Foster-Jenner family, most guys won't have any preconceived positive notions about you and therefore will not overlook the mistakes you make on first dates. You become a drunk mess and tell your date you hate his big nose? No second date. You say you're in between jobs and go on an angry rant about how much of an ugly cunt your old boss was? No second date. You ask if your date wants to do a key bump under the table and proceed to do so by yourself even after he says "no thanks"? No second date. We don't judge, but the only thing this bro will propose is a quick BJ in the taxi on the way to the club.

Sure, there are exceptions to every rule, but we're not fucking here to tell stories about your friend's cousin's camp friend whose first date ended in sex in a club bathroom and now she's engaged. We're here to talk about you, the rule (a term that was pretty useful in *He's Just Not That Into You* but then negated when they threw out all their valuable dating advice and dubbed Ginnifer "the exception." Ugh.), who should not be doing any of the aforementioned things with a guy you're just getting to know because this aforementioned girl is a straight-up mess. And the rule is that messes are not ready to date.

> "I made out with a homeless guy by accident . . . he was really tan, he had no shoes on. I just thought it was like, his thang, you know? I was like, 'He's probably in a band.'"
>
> —Amy Schumer

Good news, though: Messes only make up about 30 percent[1] of the ill-dating-prepared population. The rest are seemingly normal people who just don't like themselves. We

---

[1] Made-up percentage. Whatevs, you get it. Most people don't have their shit together.

know what you're thinking: *EW! Lame mom advice. If I wanted to be told to get my shit together I'd return my dad's calls about wanting to go over his credit card statement together.* But don't stop reading, Betch. The reason why therapists and feminists and RuPaul repeatedly ask, "How can you expect anyone to love you if you don't love yourself?" is because it's absolutely true. Sure it sounds like something a girl who likes PB&J–white-bread sandwiches with the crusts cut off would say, but it's a fact.

If you don't have your shit together enough to *genuinely* believe that you are fucking amazing and that any guy is lucky to have you, then going on dates is a complete waste of your time. I mean, one of the cornerstones of being a betch is not just *knowing* you're the hottest thing in the room, but *believing* you are even if you're not. Fake it till you make it, as they

> "So you agree, you think you're really pretty?"
> —Regina George

say. But you can only fake it for so long. There comes a point when you are living a lie and are still consistently dateless and unhappy. So what do you do? Simple. Actually get your shit together, obvs.

GETTING YOUR SHIT TOGETHER: IT'S LIKE SEPHORA FOR THE SOUL

There are so many reasons why girls hate themselves. Too fat. Too skinny. Your nail beds suck. The list goes on. But no matter how much money you spend at NARS, there's no amount of makeup that will cover up your insecurities. Unless you tackle these fuckers from inside out you'll never be as happy as you want to be and actually could be.

> *"Carol! Get your shit together, Carol!"*
> —Annie from Bridesmaids

Are we saying that you must get rid of ALL of your insecurities in order to find love? No, but at least identify the main one. Think of it as the Ed Sheeran to your Taylor Swift. It follows you around even though it's like, really unattractive but for some reason you can't stop listening to everything it says. Be brave, and kick that ginger out of your head for good.

The Physical

Let's start with the most obvious and most common reason you may hate yourself: Weight. Here's an example: Melissa McCarthy. That betch is so funny, but she's also so overweight. We know it, she knows it, and her husband knows it. Melissa McCarthy has said that she has lost weight before but she just wasn't as happy as she was with those pounds on. Whether that's a bullshit excuse to continue eating mac and cheese for breakfast or not, soak its wisdom in. She's a successful woman because she is actually happy with who looks back at her from the mirror. Of course we don't actually know her current state of happiness, but she couldn't have gotten to where she is now without extreme confidence and a solid sense of humor about explosive diarrhea.

Now let's take you as the example. Unlike Melissa, when you look in the mirror you think that if your double chin gets any bigger it will need its own Gmail account. You're constantly upset that you can't dress as chic as you would like. Sure you dress like Paris now, but you *could* dress like Nicole. And, you're constantly fidgeting and adjusting your clothes like a life-threatening tic. This kind of negative energy doesn't fly in the dating world. Guys will pick up on your insecurities faster than they'll say "I'll just pull out." In order for guys to appreciate you for you, you first need to figure out how to treat and love your body like it's a temple, or an iPhone before the new version comes out and you stop giving a shit about cracking your screen.

That said, a central tenet of being a betch is being the hottest version of yourself and always making sure your look says what you want it to say. That is, "I give a shit about how I present myself and I want people to be intimidated and envious of me." If you think you're fat, lose weight. If you think your nose sucks, get a nose job. If you think your style sucks, read a fucking magazine and go shopping.

Don't bitch about how being fat means no one will love you and then order cheese fries. It's all about identifying what it is that bothers you about yourself and then attacking that issue head on. Even excuses like "I can't afford a gym membership" don't work because you can always work harder, take a night shift somewhere, read your company's health insurance policies more carefully, and finagle yourself a monthly membership somewhere. Equinox isn't the only one to "make you do it." Plus, doing crunches in your apartment is like, free.

Shit Crazy Bitches Do: Play the Victim

We all know the girl who plays the victim when it comes to anything that requires self-improvement and self-motivation. *Ugh I just can't get up before work to go to the gym, I need sleep!; I think I have ADD, I can never concentrate on any* Times *articles; Honestly, I think I'm just allergic to vegetables at this point.* This girl exists and is very annoying because in the same sentence she'll say *I'm getting fat...I never know what's going on in the news...I eat so hashtag unclean.* The victimized betch is the worst because she will announce her issues to everyone and it's like, A) we don't fucking care and B) you're clearly lazy. The thing about laziness is that it's totally okay to be lazy, you just have to own it. Yeah we can't get up in the morning at five a.m. to run, most sane people can't. The difference is that we forgo quality Bravo & couch time to do like, one hundred squats after work. It takes skill to be a betch the right way, and this girl has it very wrong. Take some responsibility for your own choices, Karen.

Every betch should pride herself on a few things she does really well. If you think you're funny, by all means be the fat funny girl and people will care less about your weight. If you think you're pretty and that's where you get your confidence, first we suggest getting another hobby because everyone eventually grows old and looks like shit and you need something to fall back on. If you think you're smart, read more. Everyone is good at something (if you can't think of anything, call your mom), and it's about drawing confidence from the shit you're good at and working to accept the shit you're decent at if you can't fix it. You can't be ugly *and* stupid. Pick a struggle.

Nicegirls and insecure people bitch about the *Victoria's Secret Fashion Show* because it makes them insanely jealous to see beautiful women being admired by the entire world. These girls are missing the point. Yes, VS models are the most beautiful women in the world, but it takes a combination of natural genetic gifts *and hard work* to stay that way. Look at Olympic athletes. Are there thousands of women bitching about not being the

> "Be yourself. Everyone else is already taken."
> —Oscar Wilde

best cross-country skiers in the world? No, because we accept that there are some things we're never going to be the best at. So do the same with your looks. Look at the models and actresses in Hollywood the same way. They are good at what they're good at, and you're good at what you're good at. You're probably smarter or funnier or chiller than them. (Probably.) Just because you're not THE most beautiful person in the world does not mean you have to get down on hotties because of their hotness. Get over your insecurities, and accept that you are unique and bring a lot of shit to the table.

The Mental

The reason we addressed the physical first is because most people think that their insecurities are entirely superficial. But in reality, even the most physical ones stem from your perception of yourself. No matter what you think your shortcoming is, whether it's your weight, the awkward length of your arms, bad breath in the morning or scoliosis, figure out how to nip it in the bud. And by "bud" we mean "your loud brain" and by "nip" we mean "telling it to shut the fuck up."

> *"My mom always used to say, 'You can't say I love you before you can say I.' And I think that sort of makes sense."*
>
> —wise betch Mindy Kaling

If you have like, real issues that are super dark, we highly suggest you go to a therapist. Not because you're helpless, but because they're super helpful. And maybe go to the kind that prescribes you shit. She'll guide you through your problems and give you a little something for the "pain." Win-win. But with many girls, their real issues stem from past relationships. And in order to get into a new one guess what you have to do? Get the fuck over it.

Betches Throughout History: Oprah Winfrey

Lots of people want to ride with you in the limo,
but what you want is someone who will take the
bus with you when the limo breaks down.

Born into deep poverty, Oprah Winfrey is now the richest self-made betch in America. Oprah has struggled with relationship issues her whole life and never got married because she has a long history of being with abusive men who made her feel insecure. CNN and *Time* have called her the "world's most powerful woman," yet Oprah has had to struggle with accepting herself after a childhood of sexual abuse. Which like, totally sucks. In an interview, she stated that she "needed everyone to like me because I didn't like myself much. So I'd end up with these cruel, self-absorbed guys who'd tell me how selfish I was, and I'd say, 'Oh thank you, you're so right' and be grateful to them. Because I had no sense that I deserved anything else."

Oprah is a great example of how even the most talented and powerful betch has insecurities and how loving yourself can't be bought. Thinking you're the shit is a lifelong journey and even if you are literally one of the richest, most powerful people in the world, you can still fall prey to defining your worth based on the opinions of others if you don't recognize your own inner greatness. You're welcome for that history lesson.

GETTING OVER YOUR EX-WHATEVER

He doesn't have to be an actual ex-boyfriend to have fucked with your head. Whether you've just gotten out of a real relationship or a pseudo one, you still committed your thoughts to one person. And now that it's over, your thoughts naturally must go elsewhere. Sure, you have an uncanny ability to talk at length about this season's Essie colors or whether Kourtney and Scott's love for one another is eternal, but your mind will eventually find its way back to the guy whom you couldn't stop thinking about a week or even a month ago. But you have to stop thinking about him before you can let yourself start thinking about someone else (besides yourself, obviously).

> "Power is being told you're not loved and not being destroyed by it."
> —Madonna

If you had it easy and had actual closure to your relationship, all you really have to do is wait. Time, Netflix, and SoulCycle heal all wounds. Embrace them. Keep reminding yourself that your breakup was for the best and that even though life sucks right now, it will be so much better later on when your mind is clear of your ex and onto better things like the hot guy you're hooking up with or the new Chanel bag your mom got you for Christmas.

The real way to get over someone you have been under for so long is to find ways to stop thinking about him. But when you do find your mind wandering into ex territory, which typically happens when your phone dies or when the Brazilian-wax technician isn't particularly talkative that day,

just let yourself go there. Allow yourself to feel sad about the situation, that you miss him, you miss having a boyfriend, blah fucking blah. A little sadness is normal, lean into it for a few minutes.

But don't ever pity yourself. You are not hopeless; you will bounce back to your normal self. Allow yourself those few minutes of sadness, but then snap out of it. Remember that you don't need to be in a relationship to be happy. Don't forget you're a betch. Don't make us look bad.

Eventually the sadness will subside and you'll be able to think clearly. Make it a point

---

THE BOYFRIEND MOURNING FORMULA

Dated under a year:

(The amount you liked him from a scale 0-5) x [0.5 (months you dated)] = weeks to get over him.

Example: You fell out of love. So you're basically over it. Zero multiplied by anything is zero. Congrats, Betch, you're ready to move on.

Second Example: You were together for 9 months, you loved him, and he broke your heart. 5x[.5(9)]=22.5 weeks, or 5–6 months. Remember this is a *maximum*. If you take longer than this, spare your friends the agony and seek professional help. Please.

One to three years:

You have six months to one year. You're allowed one month to wallow in your own self-pity, but that's it. Use the rest of this time of mourning to get back to your old self.

Over three years:

You have one year and that's it. Okay MAYBE one and a half depending on the dramatic nature of the breakup. Just remember, Botox can't stop your eggs from aging.

to go out when you would have typically stayed in with him. If you had a favorite restaurant at which you two always ate, go find an even better restaurant and make a fucking new memory with your besties. Fuck, we feel like sad pathetic losers even writing this. But it's fine, because being depressed over a guy is a super pathetic sad and loser-y state to be in. Once you are able to look back and laugh at just how sad and pathetic you were during those long weeks or months (hopefully not years, time is the only thing you can't ever get back) then congrats because you are so over it.

Other signs you are over it: Hearing his name and not getting a weird nauseating feeling in the pit of your stomach. Good sign. Seeing him in public without peeing your pants. Another good sign.

You may also be over it if you go on a date with someone and not once even think of your ex. But by date, we don't mean a one-night stand. Sure, go out and have sex with a stranger, we don't discourage it. But don't assume that just because you fucked someone else, you're through the mourning process. Fuck for yourself, don't do it out of revenge or sadness. Because eventually the sex will end (probably too quickly) and you will go back to the rut from which you came (or more likely, didn't come).

However, if you didn't have closure to your relationship, that's an entirely different fucked-up playing field. This guy either ghosted you or never really gave you a concise, believable answer as to why he ended things. When this happens you have to make your own closure, which is about as easy and exciting as a juice cleanse or having a conversation with a cabdriver. Lucky for you, we have a handy guide for you to get over this loser.

The name of the game is Replay, Reconsider, and Repeat. (Yes, it's a play on Lather, Rinse, and Repeat. Great observation, are you like a Mensa scholar?) Unless you're dirty AF, the goal of a hair-shower (not to be confused with a body-shower, which you should do daily) is to get rid of the dirt and oils that have accumulated on your scalp and hair throughout the day(s). Now think of that dirt you're removing like the guy you're seeing. If you can get rid of him with just one rinse, congrats. But if you can't, keep repeating, Betch. He's bound to get out of your hair eventually.

Step One: Replay

Replay the relationship in your head. But instead of looking at it from your biased and slightly fantasized perspective, look at it from his. Don't be too hard on yourself, but imagine what he was thinking during each conversation or situation that you think may have taken part in your relationship's demise. When you were saying, "I'm having a birthday party Saturday, you should stop by if you want," is it possible he heard, "I want you to meet all my friends and celebrate a life milestone with me, and I'm just tricking you into a relationship"?

Step Two: Reconsider

Now that you've seen his perspective, it's time to be realistic and reconsider the situation. Delve deeper into what the actual truth of each situation is. Only then will you uncover what was actually wrong with the relationship and your communication. Here, even though it hurts, try to be as real as you can. Maybe after some consideration you realized that you didn't really know him, and he didn't know you at all. You even asked your friends what they thought of him and they're like, *What's he look like again?* Perhaps you were obsessed with the idea of him and not actually him. You know that saying that goes "there's your side, his side, and the truth"? Well the goal of this process is to see the truth. You're not a forty-five-year-old alcoholic homemaker from the 1950s; you don't need to lie to yourself.

Step Three: Repeat

Repeat this until you come to the inevitable conclusion that you two just weren't right for each other and, more important, he wasn't right for you. So whatever happened during whatever period of time you were dating eventually ends up irrelevant and you accept the fact that you don't even need to hear his side of the story because your version is about one billion times more profound than any bullshit he will have to say.

You're a betch, so you're pretty fucking smart, or at least smart enough to figure out that guys are pretty fucking stupid. As long as your reasoning isn't entirely delusional (again, lying to yourself isn't cute and is instead marginally psychotic), then you'll be able to get over him 100 percent of the time. Unless he like, died. Then take comfort in the fact that at least you weren't dumped and like, see a real therapist.

What Would Karen Do?

The complete opposite. She will use this time to dwell on how perfect his jawline is while rereading every text conversation the two of them ever had. She will then google "how to hack into Snapchat's database to recover selfies of ex-boyfriend." After she sees Results Not Found, she will continue to talk about him until her friends kindly tell her to stop bitching about that bro, he was an asshole and never liked you. She will storm away, feeling offended and over it for about five minutes. When she gets home she'll troll Tinder until she finds him, take a screenshot, send it to him and say, *I CAN'T BELIEVE YOU'VE MOVED ON SO FAST. DIDN'T I MEAN ANYTHING TO YOU!?!?* He will not respond. She'll think, *he prob just didn't get the text!*

HOW TO GET YOUR SHIT TOGETHER, UGH

If getting over your ex isn't an issue for you, but dating continues to be as unpleasant as sex with Jonah Hill, then you have to stop and consider another course of action. You don't have to consider being a lesbian just yet; you just have to try to understand why what you've been doing isn't working out.

Are you just meeting losers? Are you meeting rich hotties who won't ask for a second date? If you feel as though you're meeting losers you should consider looking somewhere else, like online. (Which we'll get to in a later chapter.) If you can't hook a second date, well then it's possible you're actually doing something wrong, which probably has a lot to do with your lack of confidence.

> "The only thing that separates us from the animals is our ability to accessorize."
> —Steel Magnolias

Warning: This might sound excruciatingly nauseating and about as painful as Ross Mathews's voice. *In order to be ready to date others you must enjoy dating yourself.* Mull it over on your vomit break.

What we mean is that if being alone doesn't make you happy then you need to immediately find the root to that unhappiness and lack of confidence and fucking fix it fast. Here's our guide to happiness, LOLZ:

1. Hearing the truth: You're a virgin who can't drive. The true test of confidence is going out with your friends and only having one to two drinks.[2] If your reaction to this suggestion is *Yeah fucking right, I'd rather slit my wrists than go out sober,* then we'd say you have some confidence issues. We didn't say go out sober, we said have just a couple of drinks, which will give you enough liquid courage to talk to outer-circle people about shit like the weather or what they do for a living. Two drinks definitely won't be enough to temporarily erase your memory that you think you have the worst skin, have just been fired, or call yourself "Fat Bastard" when you look in the mirror. If you notice general signs of a lack of self-confidence, it's definitely time to face them. You'll never get a second (or first) date if you can't even fathom someone wanting to go on one with you.

Warning signs include: Lying to your friends about the guys you're sleeping with; not wanting to participate in social group activities; an inability to look in a mirror when trying on clothes; getting really defensive about trivial things, etc.

2. Accepting the truth: That was way harsh, Tai. Pinpoint the exact thing that is standing in the way of your happiness. You probably do this all day already, but take a minute and *think about yourself.* This time, don't concentrate on what's stressing you out or what you're going to have for dinner. Instead, try to identify what it is that you really don't like about yourself. It won't be hard. If there's a bunch of things on this list, try to address each one. The hardest one

---

[2] By no means do we suggest this as a way of life. This is simply a test. Please continue to get fucked up with your besties.

to fix is almost always the reason why you feel shitty about the other ones.

Examples of woes include: Too slutty, too drunk, over-weight, unemployed, huge bitch, etc.

3. Breaking it all down: It all boiled down to one con-clusion, I was just totally clueless. Once you've figured out what the issue is, make a plan to rid yourself of it. This advice applies to how you should act when you're being pur-sued, and with a diet. Just like you wouldn't build Chipotle Day into your Juice Cleanse, you shouldn't accept anything less than committing fully from yourself. **Remember:** Noth-ing that's worth the effort is easy.

Examples of plans include: Vowing to stop sleeping with random guys; taking half shots instead of full shots; get-ting on a real diet; calming the fuck down, etc.

4. Realization: I am totally butt-crazy in love with Josh. At this point you see that people are positively reacting to your changes, saying things like "Hey, you haven't cried at a party in a while!" or "Ever since you started having juices for lunch, you've really dropped weight." This reinforcement will only help you continue to do what you're doing. If you get stuck or fuck up it's totally fine. Don't beat yourself up and keep going. If you fall off the treadmill, do you get back on? Probably not, because that was probably really fucking em-barrassing and you had to flee the gym immediately. But met-aphorically speaking you should. This is your life, and it's not casual. Take it as seriously as you take buying a new Louis

Vuitton bag or committing to summer weekends in Montauk: Super serious.

Examples of positive reinforcement include: Not wondering if you're pregnant; remembering things that took place after ten p.m.; getting compliments on how great you look; people coming to you for advice because they now think you give a shit about them, etc.

> *"Don't let the haters stop you from doing your thang."*
> —Kevin Gnapoor

What Are Men Attracted To?
by Head Pro

Fuck, that's a dumb question to ask. We're not starting off on a good note, you and I. It's not that it's a dumb thing to wonder, per se, it's just that asking "what are guys attracted to?" is like asking "what do Dalmatians think of season two of *True Detective?*" Illogical. People ask it as though, over millions of years of human existence, we've somehow managed to overlook a handful of secret factors that, once unlocked, will make the opposite sex want to see us naked. People really behave this way, too—picture every Internet ad you've ever not clicked on promising "one weird trick to get rid of bunions," or whatever the fuck.

If there were such a thing as a checklist for things men found universally attractive and I had it in my possession, I'd charge you 20 percent of your lifetime earnings and viewing rights to the first bone sesh between you and the Mr. Perfect I helped you land. Instead, the few things that men do find universally attractive tend to relate to your body, over which you have very little control. For instance, recent research has demonstrated that when shown images of various female body types, men overwhelmingly preferred shapes where the butt met the lower back at an angle of precisely 45.5 degrees. Until one of the Kardashians is bold enough to popularize elective spinal realignment surgery, you're shit out of luck. But let's be real: It's probably only a matter of time until Kylie capitalizes on that.

The good news is that for all the worrying you do about how your boobs look, whether anyone's seen you in that outfit before, etc., the way men view women is shockingly predictable—for as many dumbasses who describe themselves as "boob guys," or "ass men," the very first thing any guy notices about a woman he's actually interested in is . . . her face. It's true! While obviously men have preferences, no guy can say with any honesty that the woman with the amazing body (but fugly face) is more attractive than the one with a pretty face, provided she has all her limbs and isn't a hunchback. The point is, your face (which you can certainly improve/maximize, see the Betches' sections on shit like makeup) is a lot more important than most of the shit you spend way more time pinching, pulling at, and fretting over in the mirror. No one's going to give a shit about your muffin top if your face looks like God was chasing the dragon when he made you.

Beyond looks, things get murky. Humor is important to guys—it's not as important that you be the one with the jokes so much as it is that you have a sense of humor at all. Your sense of humor is, on a larger scale, the way in which you convey your values and worldview. I've never had a girl write to me to say her boyfriend is perfect but unfunny, nor has a girl ever written to say she finds her boyfriend hilarious but detestable in every other way. If you're with a guy who seems likeable enough, but you simply cannot find it within yourself to laugh at his decade-old Chuck Norris "facts" and *Old School* quotes, well, that's probably going to put him off—which is a good thing for you. If you don't share his sense of humor, there are likely a lot of other things you don't see eye to eye on. Actually, if anyone you meet still responds to the question of plans on Sunday with "I don't know, I don't know if we'll have enough time," that's a good sign to walk away slowly and call the fucking authorities.

Self-reliance is also a big thing. When guys complain about girls being "clingy," girls hear that as wanting to spend too much time together. That's not really the case—what guys call "clinginess" is really when a woman can't seem to do anything alone, things that make him wonder how you survived before you met him. Can you feed yourself? Can you keep your apartment livable without a maid? Can you perform routine tasks and run errands without accompaniment? Do you have a social life, ideally one that at least tangentially intersects with his? Do you have your own hobbies and interests? Got any friends? It's true that guys do tend to enjoy taking on that "provider/protector" role, but there's a bright line between "provider" and "babysitter." No guy wants the burden of constantly being the source of your stability or your good time.

These are just the biggest, most obvious boxes that men want to check off within the first few moments/days of meeting someone—beyond that, guys' individual quirks/preferences are as diverse as a college admissions brochure. That's why, rather than drive yourself fucking batshit trying to be everything to everyone, you should attempt to cultivate and sell the very best version of yourself. That is, make the most of what you have physically, be true to who you are and how you see the world, and make an effort to have interests outside of work and Instagram. There's a term for people who can't manage those simple things—we call them "VH1 reality-show contestants."

Shit Girls Care About
(That Guys Don't Even Notice)

Ever notice how girls will list someone like Nicole Richie or Rachel Zoe as their "girl crush," but guys didn't even hear what you said because they're too busy gawking at Kate Upton's jugs? It's because of something called "girl cute," or little shit that girls really care about that guys never notice. Of course, you're free to care about whatever gets your motor running, but in a dating context it might be helpful to know what kind of shit guys will notice, and what will go right over most of our heads. Stuff like . . .

He'll notice . . .	. . . But he absolutely won't notice
Hair basics—up, down, long, short, curly, straight, color.	Anything else. Whether it's the trendiest haircut of the year, whether you got a $400 dye job, you spent twenty minutes teasing it, etc.
Whether your clothes fit improperly, or if you're going for something obvious (e.g., super revealing, intentionally prudish).	Trends, subtle coordination efforts, tricks to hide parts of your body you don't like (which is actually a good thing so good job), and designer labels.

He'll notice . . .	. . . But he absolutely won't notice
Full-on clown makeup, maybe.	Literally anything else about your makeup. Ask any asshole who says he prefers a "natural" look without realizing that it takes a lot of makeup to look like you're not wearing any.
If you're wearing shoes at all, if your shoes are COMPLETELY inappropriate for the weather (e.g., sandals in January). If you have some cool workout kicks, guys might comment on those.	If your shoes are expensive or cheap, on-trend or last season. If he does notice this shit you should ask yourself if you really want to be this guy's beard or, worse, date someone who dresses better than you.

You probably get the point. Apply the same rules for jewelry, accessories, etc. In general, guys have no sense of context for your appearance—we see you in a vacuum, as you stand before us. In a way, this is a good thing! While you might get annoyed that a special someone didn't notice that the soles of your shoes matched your eye shadow or whatever, it means you should continue to dress the way you want *for you* and not for anyone else. Or at least not for the guy's sake—whatever weird infighting girls have over this stuff is light-years beyond my understanding.

Dear Head Pro,

My girlfriends and I are noticing a lame trend:
Our careers are great for our wallets, but not for
boyfriends. Hear me out. I'm a successful young
woman in NYC and there is a good chance I make just
as much, if not more money than the guys I tend to
gravitate toward, i.e., anyone with a legit stable career.
I watch as much ESPN as I do Bravo and despite
spilling my shit to someone I don't know via e-mail,
I consider myself to be one of the "normal ones." I
don't by any means flaunt my money, but I do present
myself nicely. I'm totes comfortable at Per Se one
second and then zip-lining through the rain forest the
next. . . . Basically, like many betches in a big city, I'm
a size 2, I went to a great school, and I'm not a total
whore, so what the fuck gives?

When men approach me, I typically have a casual yet
proper interaction with them and they're hooked! We
then go on a date and dabble in career, family, and
travel talk and before I can even pay for dessert (a
lady always offers to pay for dessert or one round of
drinks), they're looking around for the next anorexic,
airhead skank to bone and me and my Prada bag are
left to hail a cab back home for a night of wine, ice
cream, and *Sixteen* fucking *Candles*, before pulling
my shit together and doing this all over again.

I don't want to dumb myself down so a dude can feel
more superior. I have no idea what the hell feeling
it is that dudes are seeking. And as fucking lame as
it sounds, the man that I am supposed to chill with
for like, ever will love me the way I am, for sure. But

whatever the hell it is that I am doing right now, is proving repellent.

Is it true? Do guys only like girls who look like anorexic bitches? Is it truly unattractive when a woman has an education? Is it gross to have a sweet career? We grow up being taught that skinny, kind, educated, pretty people are the only ones who end up with love, happiness, and money. Well I am happy, I have money, but my shit gets lonely when I see couples running around all over the damn place.

Sorry for sounding like an idiot,
Betch in the City

Dear Betch in the City,

Well, you don't sound like an idiot, so no need to beat yourself down. However, I am sensing something of a self-perception issue. You may be the most interesting girl alive, but your description of yourself reads like a parody of a terrible Match.com profile (ESPN/Bravo, Per Se/zip-lining, name-dropping your passé bag manufacturer). Maybe cool it with that, a little.

Anyway, in the interest of brevity, I think three things are happening:

1. You basically admitted this yourself: There's nothing special about you. You're just like many other "Betches in a big city," as you say. What you're learning is that being "skinny, kind, educated, pretty" only nets you an invite to the

dance that is "love, happiness, and money"; it doesn't guarantee you a dance partner. Tell me more about this zip-lining, or what specifically you like to watch on Bravo or ESPN—set yourself apart in some way, however small.

2. Leading with how awesome and (un)exceptional your life is doesn't exactly make clear how dating you would either offer him anything or offer him the opportunity to improve your life, especially when you want to date like-minded men. People want to feel needed. They want to feel like the bond they share with you creates something greater than the sum of its parts. Though you're justified in being proud of your success, maybe stick to more subjective topics that offer room for the guys you date to offer some of their own perspective.

3. Truth be told, guys don't give a shit about a girl's success, at least not initially. Of course ambition and goals are important long-term, but no one says, "one of the things I find hot about her is how well she's doing career-wise." I mean, guys will hit on the cashier at Chipotle if she's hot and looks like she might have a story to tell, for fuck's sake. People really only tolerate talk of work from their friends, family, and other loved ones. Until you're one of those things, you're not doing yourself any favors by making it seem like your job is all you have going for you.

So no, guys aren't only attracted to "anorexic bitches," and there's nothing "gross" about an education or a career. And no, by no means should you dumb yourself down, not for a guy or anyone else. It's more that no one wants to date what you present as a walking humanoid combination of a resume and a credit card statement. There are better ways to use your success and ego to your advantage— have a little mystery about you. You should make them *want* to find out these things about you, not beat them over the head with it on date #1.

Disinterested kisses,
Head Pro

SPARK NOTES

If you couldn't pay attention to anything we just wrote because you were busy drying your nails or concentrating on your tan, it's okay. We've been there. Life's hard when you're a betch and poss not/def have ADD. So let's break down what happened in this chapter.

Before you even start to date, you need to make sure you're ready. But there's a catch. Being ready doesn't only mean being over the last guy you were with (which requires a certain element of emotional intelligence, introspection, and not being a fucking Karen). What you really need is to have your shit together. You need to be confident with your hot bod and your brain. And if you're not into your bod and brain, work on it. You need to believe this phrase when you say it to yourself: *I'm totally chill being single but having a boyfriend sounds like it could be fun. Who wouldn't want to date me? After all, I am the shit.* Only then are you really ready to enter into the big, bad dating world.

2

So Now I'm Like, Really Pretty, Where Do I Find Him?

Getting Out There

Now that you know you're hot shit, it's time to go out there and get him. It's important to remember that the goal of any activity or experience should never be to find a boyfriend. When you give off the vibe that you're desperate for love, men are repelled by it because it makes you seem like you have a mission that has more to do with checking a "boyfriend" box off your list of shit to do than meeting someone truly amazing with whom you just happen to want to spend a lot of time.

> "If you don't have a valentine, hang out with your girlfriends, don't go looking for someone. When it's right, they'll come to you."
> —Carmen Electra

As Bethenny Frankel says, going out with the mind-set that you need to meet a guy is like going to a casino and betting with your rent money. Scared money never wins and scared dating just reeks of desperation. Your goal in all your activities should be to have a good time with whomever you're with and if you happen to meet someone, that's great, if not then whatevs. No one wants to date the girl who seems desperate to settle down. It's lame, and it shows you don't have much else going on in your life. Ideally you want to meet someone while doing things you love. If you're doing you, you'll attract guys that are impressed by your independence and fun attitude. You want to meet someone during your life's journey, not have the journey be just checking items off your to-do list to accomplish the goal of meeting someone.

That being said, you can meet guys like, literally anywhere. I mean, there are three billion of them in the world and probably at least two hundred acceptable ones. Besides the chance encounter of meeting a guy on line at Just Salad (which is pretty rare in a city like Manhattan, where, when anyone talks to you soberly, your first instinct is to clutch your pepper spray) there's a shit-ton of casual ways to run into the opposite sex while actually doing things you enjoy.

SO WHERE ARE ALL THE MEN?

Sober Activities: If you like sports, join a coed intramural sports team. If you actually like helping other people and planning events, join a charity committee. If you like skiing, plan ski houses with friends of friends. If you like reading 50 *Shades of Grey,* get a life. Just kidding, join a book club or some other activity that involves something that you actually like doing that has nothing to do with men. That way, you'll wind up meeting guys who have a lot in common with you without the pressure of being forced to decide if you like each other immediately. Summerhouses in places like the Hamptons and Nantucket (or whatever local lake you have where you live) are great for bringing together extended friend groups and introducing you to people you can safely assume are normal by association.

Work: Dating someone you work with is usually frowned upon because if things go sour, the awkwardness and discomfort is surrounding you five days a week and at every office happy hour. Plus, your office goggles almost always make the only moderately decent-looking bro in the office look like Ryan Gosling by comparison to his middle-aged balding counterparts. No doubt spending a ton of time with someone in that close of a setting leads itself to a ton of hookup opportunities, but it's almost always best to not go there. I promise you that the Christmas party make-out sesh will not lead to marriage. Instead, it'll lead to you having to avoid questions from your office mates about how big Jason's penis is for the next three to five years.

One exception to this rule is meeting men you work with peripherally or meet through work events, which can actually be a great way to meet people who have a lot in common with your work interests without the horror of having to see them every day. Be careful with client-relationships, but keep an eye out for tangentially work-associated people.

Getting Set Up: Getting set up can be a disaster or a miracle depending on who you let be your fairy godmother/yenta. The ideal matchmaker should be someone who has high standards for you and knows you well enough to know that someone shorter than five feet ten and employed at Equinox is simply not acceptable. They should know the kind of personality traits you value and the shit you can let slide.

Never trust your grandma for a setup because she is half blind and therefore can't see the receding hairline. Also, old people tend to see all young people as attractive both because of flawed vision and an idealization of youth. Likewise, your mom's ideal match for you will likely have more to do with his 401K and less to do with how well he tans in the summer months so unless your mom is cool as fuck, leave the setups to your friends and well-connected coworkers.

> *"I want a man who is kind and understanding. Is that too much to ask of a millionaire?"*
> —Zsa Zsa Gabor

Bars/Clubs: The chances of you finding someone to make out with at a bar or a club are far greater than you finding someone who is boyfriend material. I mean, very few people find meaningful relationships with a guy who grabbed their ass during a dance floor hookup. Having said that, it does happen—on rare occasions—that a guy you meet at one of these places asks you on a date because your drunken coordination of the Uber was just so impressive and he can tell from your six-inch stilettos that you're going to make a great mom someday. Use your best judgment when deciding whether to accept.

Making Sure You Don't Ditch Your Friends

No one likes the annoying bitch who ditches her friend at the first sign of male attention. Not only does this signal that you are flaky as fuck, it signals to the guy that he's more important to you than your friends which is not exactly playing hard to get upon first encounter.

At this stage of the game when you go out it should be to enjoy your friends' company. If you happen to meet a great guy while out, that's just the icing on top of the cake you shouldn't be eating. Going out just to meet guys is super sad. Go dancing with your friends and do activities you'd enjoy whether or not guys are in your presence, and you will attract guys who are attracted to your essence, not the person you're pretending to be.

Remember that casual bars are usually better than clubs for meeting decent guys and that if you do want to meet someone while socializing at a drinking venue, it's best to not be totally blackout. It's one thing to exchange numbers with a guy you got buzzed off a few vodka sodas with at a chic lounge but it's quite another to be so plastered at 1 Oak that all this guy remembers about you is your nice ass and the fact that you're obsessed with grinding to "Drunk in Love."

What Would Karen Do?

Karen is desperate to date, so she only goes out when she is under the impression that there will be many single, eligible guys in her vicinity. When she's out with her friends she's ignoring them so she can eye-fuck any bro in her line of vision and will immediately ignore everyone around her when she starts talking to a guy. If a guy she's talking to tries to exit the conversation, she keeps asking him questions and follows him around the bar. No matter the truth of her encounter with this guy, she will invariably tell all of her friends that he is "obsessed with her" and "wouldn't leave her alone" when it's clear to see that he's trying to escape her. Don't be a Karen, always leave the conversation at its peak so as to leave a guy wanting more.

If you've been around the block and these things are simply not working for you, it might be time to look into on-line dating . . .

ONLINE DATING: IT'S ONLY WEIRD IF YOU MAKE IT WEIRD

The topic of online dating is very much debated. Not really publicly, but like, a lot at Sunday brunch. Sure it's super fun to tell horror stories of your experiences of talking with guys on Tinder but when it comes to a successful match, do you feel weird saying you met online when someone asks your story?

Since we googled this one statistic that says that one in five relationships start online, we're pretty positive the stigma attached to online dating is disappearing faster than Shia LaBeouf's relevance. Sure we still feel a little weird when we tell someone we're going on a date with someone we met on Match but it's definitely not that bad anymore. In an ideal world, you meet a guy because he saves you from getting hit by a cab and immediately takes your breath away. But this is real life, not a shitty Jennifer Lopez movie, so do whatever you have to do to stay in the game. This includes online dating.

The simple fact is: Everyone's doing it. And by "everyone" we mean just a lot of people you know, and once you see a lot of people you know doing something questionable, like instagramming their food or going back to school for a master's degree, it becomes kind of cool.

> "All you need is for one person to think you're cool, and you're in. Everyone else will be scared to question it."
> —Josie Grossie's brother, *Never Been Kissed*

Now, we are not saying online dating is actually cool. It's just not uncool. What online dating does that meeting people in real life doesn't is it allows you to branch out without leaving your normal routine. Now you are able to "meet" people outside of your immediate network without having to do something arduous like go to religious services or like, volunteer at a soup kitchen. The ease and accessibility instantly increase your chances of meeting someone you would have otherwise never met, which in turn could increase your chances of meeting your next boyfriend without having to interrupt your carefully cultivated life. The trick is to go about it casually. Don't stop meeting people in real life. Like becoming a fashion blogger, online dating is something you do on the side. Treat it as such.

We take issue with complacency in "dating culture" that says it's okay to just hook up with someone who has never taken you out to dinner and hoping that one day it'll become a real thing. *WRONG*. Online dating eliminates that pseudo-date/hang-out shit and forces the guy to ask you on a real date, in public, because you two haven't met before and he can't just run into you at a frat party when you're too drunk to know better.

Side note: First dates that aren't in public are scary and you should not go on them because you will probably be murdered.

However, there are cons of looking for bae online. The biggest one is relying on pictures and meeting someone you've never met before. This is scary fucking shit. What if he like, only used pics from 2014 when he was really on his workout grind and has since gained back an entire chin?! What if he shows up and is about five inches shorter than the height he selected in his profile!? What if he only makes five figures a year? What if he has a super-thick Scottish accent and you don't understand a word he's saying because he sounds like Shrek!?!? Don't worry, you're not alone.

These are called the HODs (Horrors of Online Dating) and they're the most terrible to experience in the moment, but the most fun to recall to your besties afterward. In order to avoid these you just have to be really good at reading and translating someone's profile and messages. Yes, this is really judgmental, but you two haven't met yet so what's the harm? Plus, you're a betch so you can be as judgmental as you want. Your weeknights are precious and you would so much rather be sitting braless binge-watching the new season of *Orange Is the New Black* than having a drink with some finance guy who has an acne problem and may or may not ask you to split the check. Hence, you need to draw some conclusions based on what they write.

On the flip side, the awful-yet-hilarious story of the guy who got so drunk he threw up all over himself and then tried to pretend someone vomited on him while he was in the restroom will be an amazing story to tell your friends at drunk brunch, and will therefore enhance your repertoire of funny shit to say, making you a more interesting and therefore more datable person over all. Moral of the story: If your life looks like a sad Instagram meme of you sitting at home watching Netflix and eating Chipotle every Thursday night, you're not going to be that interesting to date. So accept that

Hinge date, get the fuck out of your apartment, and go make some ridiculous memories.

Where to Online Date

Since online dating sites are more diverse than the cast of *SNL,* we figured you don't want to jump into those murky waters without our help. So we've broken down all the sites worth knowing about. Anything not covered here can safely be ignored.

Online dating comes in three forms: Shit you have to pay for, shit you don't have to pay for, and apps. First we'll cover the sites you have to pay for because, like they say, nothing good ever comes free and without an extensive background check.

Shit You Have to Pay For

Because they cost money, these sites require a little bit more commitment. The positive is that the guy might be actually trying to find a girlfriend, but the negative is he could be trying a little too hard to find a girlfriend. No one wants to date some desperate lonely loser who will pay thousands of dollars to find a wife. If we did, we'd be mail-order brides. There's a fine line between a catch who's casually online dating and a sad weirdo who is a hop, skip, and jump from finding comfort in the arms of hookers if this whole OkCupid thing doesn't work out. Keep in mind that you'll likely get what you pay for. The free sites are loaded with freaks. The pay sites tend to have people who are a little more serious about meeting people, rather than using a dating site as a platform to articulate their political beliefs and *Lord of the Rings*–based fantasies.

Match.com: Seems legit enough. Do you love BuzzFeed quizzes? Match.com has all the personality tests of Buzz-Feed, but with like, half the fun and twice the pressure.

eHarmony.com: Pretty sure that's for old people, right? I always see that grandpa bro with the white hair on those commercials and I'm like, why would I want your wrinkly face promoting love, sex, and relationships?

HowAboutWe.com: This site is ideal if you're an outside-the-box-thinking overachiever whose idea of getting to know someone includes spending all day with them, devouring fucking baguettes at Eataly or going on a scavenger hunt in a nearby national park. If so, by all means knock yourself out.

JDate/ChristianMingle: Many success stories on this one, also many Andy Andersons who "bump into you" near your apartment and walk with you to work the next day, despite living in a completely different part of town.

Perfect for the betch whose religion is important to her or the Jewish American betch with the overbearing mother who won't stop bothering her to "meet a nice Jewish boy and settle down already because I need grandchildren immediately even though I'm only fifty-six years old."

Grouper: This company coordinates a blind group date between you and two of your besties and a group of three guy friends. Grouper picks the place and pays for the first drink (but not really because you paid for the one-time service). The date can be extremely awkward, totally fine, or a complete shitshow. In most scenarios there's one person, guy and/or girl, left with the unattractive friend. (Gentle tip: If you don't see the ugly friend sitting with you, the ugly friend is you.) After the date you almost always remain single and now have an extra Facebook friend whose updates are more annoying than your mom's.

InterracialPeopleMeet: Perfect for the Jewish girl who's looking to get back at her aforementioned overbearing mother.

SeekingArrangement: We're all for getting older guys to pay for shit, but if you're going to make a profile on Seeking Arrangement you might as well just send out your resume to an escort service. Let's be real, this shit is "a mutually beneficial relationship" like A1 on *Breaking Bad* was "just a car wash."

Sites You Don't Have to Pay For

OkCupid: Maybe you're not sure you need to fully commit to online dating, maybe you're Hannah Horvath and you just got cut off, maybe you're an unpaid intern. Whatever the reason, OkCupid doesn't require a monthly membership, and the layout doesn't look like complete shit, so that's a plus.

The downside: It gives you a lot of work in the form of a fuck-ton of useless questions such as, "Do you believe morality is universal or relative?" and "How do you feel about documentaries?" If we wanted to do that much work we would've applied to grad school.

Plenty of Fish: Good if you hate doing work (see: OkCupid), bad if you're not good at writing paragraphs about yourself without any prompts whatsoever. For whatever reason, guys on POF seem less likely to use corny pickup lines. Maybe because guys on POF are smart enough to know that shit doesn't work? Or maybe they're too lazy to think of puns? Unclear. The bad news is the homepage looks more chaotic than Hiroshima in 1945. I can't tell which are my potential matches and which are PornHub ads . . . *Is Chad in Decatur who wants to show me a good time the real deal, or . . . ?*

Zoosk: What the actual fuck is Zooșk? Literally the login page just looks like a more racially diverse version of Guess Who.

Apps

Tinder: Not so much a dating app as it is a "meet up for one drink and then shadily fuck in his backseat in a parking lot" app. If you're looking to go on actual dates, be prepared to weed through a lot of people because the number of dudes looking for relationships on Tinder is approximately equal to the amount of people who use VHS.

Happn: For people you want to make sure work in a major city and aren't secretly living at home with their parents. It pulls a list of guys you "cross paths" with, a.k.a. someone who frequents a Manhattan Starbucks. *Soooo much in common.*

It's kind of annoying because it doesn't give you matches so you have to weed through all the people that look like they want to kill you, but it's also kind of nice in that there's an endless amount of dudes who live and work around you to scroll through when you're waiting in line for your iced coffee. I mean there's no way you're raising your head up from looking at your texts long enough to actually notice them standing next to you in the actual Starbucks.

Coffee Meets Bagel: At first we thought this was some sort of Jewish sex ring . . . just us? Okay. Then we watched *Shark Tank,* saw the founders, and were profoundly confused. Anyway, you only get one match per day and, just like your birth control, you get it at twelve p.m. sharp, which is also perfect if you're the Bat-Shit-Crazy Betch (BSCB) who has less self-control than high James Franco at a Domino's about texting all the guys in her phone book.

Hinge: Imagine a world where you don't have to ask your friends to set you up, because an app does it for you. Betches, that app is Hinge. This app has everything: Some questions about your preferences, the same swipe format as Tinder, a whole lot of your personal information, and some guys that you assume are normal because you once met them at your camp friend's pregame in 2013.

Bumble: The idea behind Bumble is that the girls have to message the guy first. The idea of making it even easier for guys to date on dating apps that already make it really insanely easy for them to date is sort of annoying. That being said, if you're looking to meet guys who are nice but maybe a little shy, and want to have a chance to stand out and not be lumped in with every other dick pic solicitor on the Internet, then this is the tool for you. Having said that, a lot of the guys on this thing are pretty hot, like questionably unreal hot.

For those of you ESL betches out there, here's a simple breakdown of what we're looking at in the online dating scene.

Dating App or Site	What It Says About the Person on It
OkCupid	"It's free so if anyone asks I can tell my friends I signed up drunk."
eHarmony	"Message me so I can tell you about my cats!"
Match	"I have a job, so I can pay for a dating website."
Tinder, Hinge, Bumble, etc.	"What? Haha, no, of course I don't take this seriously!" [swipes right]
JDate, ChristianMingle, etc.	"I have very judg-y parents."
Plenty of Fish	"Yeah . . . I'm just desperate."

Okay, you've got your profile set up. Now what? Discerning conversations take practice and a conversational partner who isn't oblivious to normal social cues. What we mean by that is: Sometimes you can tell a lot more about a guy by what he *doesn't* say than what he does say. It's important to read between the lines. As in, if all of his pictures are of him and his grandma and pet lizard, he is obviously a loser.

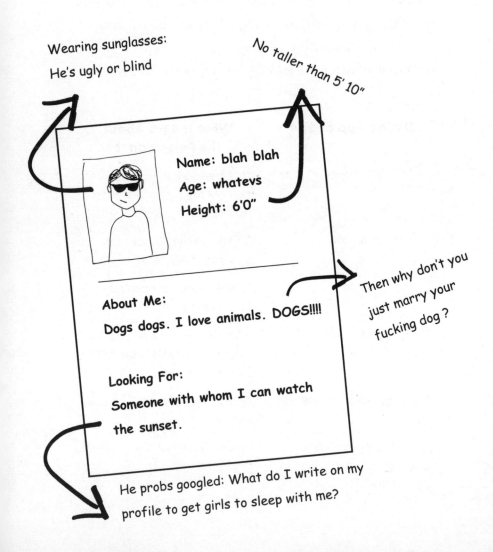

Wearing sunglasses:
He's ugly or blind

No taller than 5' 10"

Name: blah blah
Age: whatevs
Height: 6'0"

About Me:
Dogs dogs. I love animals. DOGS!!!!

Then why don't you just marry your fucking dog?

Looking For:
Someone with whom I can watch the sunset.

He probs googled: What do I write on my profile to get girls to sleep with me?

His profile:

Wears sunglasses in all his pictures. Read: He's probably a lot less attractive when he takes them off.

Wears a hat in every picture. Read: Dude's bald.

All pictures are of him alone taken with a webcam. Read: He doesn't have any friends.

6'0." Read: He's 5'10."

5'8." Read: He could be an honest 5'8," but he's most likely 5'5."

Shirtless bathroom mirror selfie. Read: Fucking run.

His opening message:

Hey what's up? I'm Jason how was your weekend? Read: This is a normal person who is interested in meeting you.

Hey I think we would make attractive children. Read: If he was trying to be funny, this guy is confident and has a sense of humor. If he wasn't, he's super creepy and you should like, make sure your address is not written anywhere on your profile.

Hi I'm Jason, I like long walks on the beach, reading Kurt Vonnegut, and walking my bulldog Cooper. I live in Murray Hill in an apartment with my 2 friends from college and I love to work out on the weekends. What's your schedule like this week? Read: This guy is prob too nice for you. The over-share is a sign of someone who doesn't really have a strong sense of humor or much experience with women.

Hey you have nice tits. What's your number? Read: BYE.

I think we have a lot in common. We should get together for drinks if you're free this week. Read: This is a bold, no-bullshit ask out. He seems super confident and doesn't really like on-line small talk. This guy could be a douche, but he could also just want to get to know you in person. This is your strongest option. Accept the date and hope it doesn't suck.

The great thing about a guy's opener is that it says a lot about him with a little information. As a general rule, look for guys who seem like they're no-bullshit and who want to take the conversation off-line fairly quickly.

Inspirational Historical Betch: Zelda Fitzgerald

It is the loose ends with which men hang themselves.

Zelda Fitzgerald was born into a wealthy Southern family and casually met F. Scott at a country-club dance. She was like, not that into him because he was mad poor and therefore friendzoned him faster than you can say "Prohibition." The two wrote letters to each other and Zelda basically told Fitz that he could go shave his back now and she was dating other bros. Desperate to impress this hottie, Fitz started writing books instead of articles and went on to write *The Great Gatsby.* Ever heard of it?

Zelda shows us that if you act like you DGAF and don't seem impressed with a guy, they will go out of their way to impress you and maybe even write the next great American novel in an effort to pay for all your shit.

Exchanging messages:

Too many questions. Read: This guy has asked you every question he can think of. Except the one you want to hear, which is *do you want to get a drink this week?* This type of messager is super frustrating, and at some point you have to stop answering. He'll get the hint and write again asking you out. If he doesn't get the message and instead sends a follow-up to his previous question you should just block him. There is literally nothing more annoying than a dude who tries to make small talk for upwards of three days before asking you out. No, I don't give a shit how your week is going. I don't even know you. I don't even ask my friends this and I like, actually sort of care about their lives.

He asks for your number too soon. Read: This is always so uncomfortable. You want to say no but you know you'll probably give it to him later. If you feel okay giving your number then go for it, but if you don't then say something like: "Ah, I'm not huge on giving out my number before talking to someone for a bit. Hope that's okayyyy." You seem normal and apprehensive, which are two good qualities for a person to have. If he brushes you off and stops responding, he's def a freak who would have sent you dick pics anyway.

He takes twenty years to respond. Read: Fuck this guy. Everyone has a life, but if he's not interested enough to respond to you within one to two days then why message you to begin with. You also have a life, but a guy who waits a week to respond isn't worth your time.

He gets to know you a little (one to two days of messages) and then asks you out. Read: This is good. Go with this.

A Note on Messaging First: This is entirely situational, and by situational we mean, the only situation in which you should do this is if there's a killer in your house and the guy coincidentally lives nearby so you need him to like, help. The other situation is that if he has texted you first three times in a row and you want to show him that you're interested and that you're not a completely horrible person.

Creating the Perfect Profile

On whichever app or site you choose, it's crucial that you portray yourself in the best yet still honest light.

Choosing pictures: The pictures you post are the most important because that's really all people have to go on when dating online. Always choose three to four photos. Two is too little, five is too many. Your main should be you alone looking super hot or like, *really* pretty. The main pic is to catch a guy's attention, look at the camera, smile, and don't include four of your hot friends in this photo. If you think a pic of you looking down reading a book is going to catch his attention then you should probably switch to LibrariansSeeking Soulmates.com. This probably doesn't exist, but if it did the small talk would be super pretentious.

The next should be a full body shot of you either cut out from a picture with your friends or a "funny" candid. *Don't post pictures of you posing alone.* It's just weird. It may have been funny in context, but it's definitely super loser-y out of it. And after that you should definitely include pictures of you looking like you do other things besides stalk Instagram and get blackout drunk. We suggest skiing, painting, or riding a horse.

A very important side note: Your pictures should be recent and at normal angles in which you do not look four sizes smaller than you are. No guy will ever say to his friends, "Yeah she totally catfished me, like forty pounds heavier than in her pics, but her personality blew me away." This only happens in romantic comedies and your dreams. You don't want to date a guy who doesn't like what you look like anyway, so why hide? If you're overweight, guys who are into that will message you. If you don't like those types of guys, go on a fucking diet. It's not science. Rule of thumb: You always want to be hotter in person than you appear in your pictures.

Writing a profile: Obviously, the profile only applies to sites that require you to write one. Either way, don't stress about it because a guy who thinks you look super hot in your pics will never say *ehhh but she's a PA, I only really date doctors*. With profiles, less is much, much more. Don't write an essay about how you felt after your parents' divorce in '02. Write the facts and one sort of funny joke. Let them know you're lighthearted and don't take this shit too seriously. You're a betch, you have other things to do besides sit around and apply for a boyfriend. Write a few lines about yourself

"Guys don't care what you do. A guy could be talking to two women at a party, and one is beautiful and just won the Nobel Prize in Literature, and the other is just slightly hotter and like, has a job interview at H&M in the morning. And 10 times out of 10, you know how that's going to go."
—Amy Schumer

and run it by a friend. If she says you sound like a delusional maniac, rewrite. Then leave it alone. See? It's simple.

So yeah, the good news is that whatever you do for a liv-

Do Guys Care About Your Job?
by Head Pro

No! Well, not really. Linking suitability as a mate to one's employment is still a distinctly masculine idea, like pretending that fantasy football is actually fun or never washing our sheets. Despite women embarking on long and fruitful careers for the better part of a century at this point, your career doesn't matter much to us in terms of how fuckable you are, the way ours do for you. You'll be very disappointed if you convince yourself your career in marketing is what makes you datable, only to discover he's been banging a tollbooth attendant behind your back.

That's not to say that you shouldn't have a job, and one you care about—ambition is a very sexy quality, and bodes well for other aspects of a potentially successful relationship. Just don't make the mistake guys do by going into a field thinking it will score you tons of prospects, or assuming you're undatable because you work in retail. It's *very* rare for a guy to shy away from a girl due to her "station" in life. I mean, a quick scan of the number of waitresses and yoga instructors among the female contestants on *The Bachelor* will clue you in to the importance most men place on things like jobs that require a bachelor's degree. When it does, it usually has more to do with her family's socioeconomic standing than what she actually does for a living.

ing probably isn't going to affect your datability, unless you're a hooker or something. And even then . . .

When it comes to online dating, you're going to inevitably wind up going on a ton of shitty dates with guys you regret having wasted an ounce of your Chanel mascara on. But dating is really a numbers game, and using the Internet to meet more men ups your chances of meeting someone you really like. It's tempting to want to come home and check out with a bottle of wine and an *Us Weekly* after a long day pretending to do work at the office, but resist that urge. You can't win if you're not in the game.

That being said, treat online dating as a fun, light distraction from your regular week. Make sure you're still maintaining your social life and don't ever cancel an actual fun event or happy hour so you can meet a stranger you met on the Internet. Treat dating like you would any other aspect of your life, casually. There will be some good times and some bad times, but the best part of going on a ton of shitty first dates is that you don't have to pay for any of them.

You've got a lot of shit going on in your life. If you happen to meet a surprisingly cute, interesting rando online whom you wouldn't have met otherwise because your resting betch face is too intimidating at the bars, online dating has worked its magic. Plus, what else are you doing on a Tuesday night?

What Guys Think of Your Profile
by Head Pro

Online dating is like signing Ellen DeGeneres to be the face of CoverGirl Cosmetics: Seemingly insane, but surprisingly effective. By now just about all of us have dabbled in online dating in one form or another, and that's great. After all, "online dating" really just means using the Internet as a way to meet people in real life. If we use the Internet for ordering groceries, takeout, and dildos, why not use it to order up someone to fuck, right? If for whatever reason it still sounds unappetizing to you, consider this: People tend not to hide their crazy on the Internet. If a guy talks about being "red pill" or "alpha" and has strong opinions about how women in the workplace are ruining things for men, he's a lot more likely to express those sentiments up front online than he is in person. It's a lot better to find these things out right away, rather than three dates in when you're chained to someone's radiator, left to contemplate the series of decisions that led you to that moment.

Most online dating seems pretty straightforward, but as with oral sex and pronouncing the word "aluminum" in the UK, people manage to fuck up the simplest things. The universe of online dating profiles is a triage room of banal biographies, uninteresting "interests," and photos of people taken during the W. administration. It's no surprise, then, that the online dating experience often leaves people feeling like they just masturbated during a church service—sullied and only half fulfilled. But your online dating experience doesn't have to suck, provided you can make your profile not suck. And you can, in fact, make your profile suck-free, provided you adhere to the following guidelines for what guys look for in online dating profiles.

Screen Name

Surprisingly, this matters. Researchers at Queen Mary University of London found that generally, screen names beginning with letters in the first half of the alphabet are more successful. Avoid words with negative connotations ("little," "chubby," etc.), and the same research showed that men are more likely to click on names containing words referencing physical attractiveness. "LawSkewlCutie" is okay, "TinyStripper91," not so much.

Pictures

You definitely want to have some, and it should go without saying that they should represent what you look like right now. People constantly try to fudge their pictures, which is dumb. Here's a secret: Unless you're planning a date with Stevie Wonder, guys will know if you lied with your pictures. As far as what goes on in those pictures, a UConn study found that women with "altered" photos (that is, enhanced by using makeup, favorable lighting, etc.) consistently scored higher in terms of attractiveness and dating desirability—so slap on some makeup. It's also a good idea to have pictures of you having a good time with other people. I would avoid, however, pictures of you surrounded by nothing but dudes. While you may feel like it shows how desirable you are, all it does is make most guys imagine you fucking each of those other guys, either one by one or in a big, delightful orgy.

Profile

Try not to be generic. For as much as women like talking about themselves, they're pretty bad at doing it in writing. Every girl's profile is something like this:

> *"I love traveling and trying new foods, but more than anything I love laughing with my friends. I'm as comfortable going out on the town as I am staying in and snuggling. I love having fun and being silly, but I have a serious side, too. I'm looking for a man who can make me laugh, support me when I cry, and be my partner in crime."*

OMG WE HAVE SO MUCH IN COMMON!!! No shit, everyone likes/is looking for those things. In trying to be broad and all-encompassing in your description, you've actually managed to say nothing. It's not the easiest thing to do, but put some effort into it. What inspires you? What gets you out of bed in the morning? What are your hobbies/interests (other than judging people)? If you don't have any passions, that's probably why you're single. Become interesting.

Your best bet is to be honest about yourself (within reason). If you're like, into zip-lining through the jungle while listening to Elton John at full volume, say that. Other, more personal things, though, are probably best kept off the Internet. If you think that Adolf Hitler was "just really misunderstood," maybe save that tidbit for later. But in general, there's nothing to be gained by portraying yourself as something you're not.

Shit Crazy Bitches Do: Write Insane Dating Profiles

You can always smell a crazy desperate girl a mile away by simply looking at her online dating bio. Phrases like "not being like other girls," "not looking for just a hookup," or "XYZ need not apply" are massive red flags that this girl is damaged and certifiable. By coming off insanely aggressive in their profiles, they appear desperate and not as though they're here to have fun and meet new people. Even if you're not looking to make new friends, your dating profile should never imply that you're here for a ring or you need to GTFO. Relax, bitch, why so serious?

When Is It Okay for Me to Hit On a Guy? by Head Pro

Guys are the ones historically charged with initiating an interaction. Believe me when I say it would be awfully nice if we could just buck convention and have girls sidling up next to us at bars instead of vice versa. And I'm sure it would be equally nice if, instead of twirling your hair around your finger until it falls off waiting for a guy to notice you, you could just roll up and be all "'sup, bro?" (clearly I have no idea what female pickup lines sound like). Sadly, this is not the case. In our little corner of the world, it's the men who do all the "hey baby"-ing, and it's rare indeed for women to be the initiators.

What the fuck, who are you to tell me my role in society, this is a free fucking country, you might be fuming, to which I say, you've got a lot of nerve getting all worked up over a book you're reading at the Starbucks inside the last surviving Barnes & Noble. But, yes, we live in a free country, and you're *technically* free to hit on guys the same way you're *technically* free to pick your nose on the subway or use the n-word in casual conversations. That doesn't mean those are good ideas, though.

But! As you may have guessed from the heading of this section, there do happen to be some times when it's okay (or even preferable) for a girl to be the one to say, "Come here often?" even if the response is "Christ, lady, this is an abortion clinic, that was totally inappropriate." Here are the times and places when you should go for it:

Time is of the essence: Any time you're somewhere where there's a legitimate chance you may never see this person again (vacation, visiting friends out of town, etc.) and if you see a guy who catches your eye but who hasn't noticed you yet, there's no harm in taking a chance. I mean, if you crash and burn, it's not like anyone you know is there to see it.

He's alone but you aren't: Real talk, a lot of guys can be intimidated by groups of women. They shouldn't be, but a lot of times men simply assume that they'll be shut down by the group. If you're failing to make it clear that you'd like him to approach, but you've exchanged some looks that indicate the interest is mutual, it's fine to break away from the herd and say hi yourself.

Any place where it's mostly men: Here's a secret—promoters don't try to fill clubs with mostly women just because they like the look of thirty women in the tiniest dresses they own; they also do it because men aren't super comfortable in a sausage fest. Male-dominated spaces are charged, tense atmospheres, like places showing big sporting events. Rejoice in having your pick of the litter, and strategically position yourself near the dude who caught your eye.

Bonus: Assuming you're also there to watch the game, you have an instant conversation topic.

Any time he's on your turf: Or, to put it another way, any time your "status" is higher than his. Obviously if you're some kind of celebrity, first of all thanks for reading, but also assume that any guy in attendance is imagining your six-foot-five, 240-pound combination-Navy-SEAL-theoretical-physicist boyfriend waiting to ambush any asshole who hits on you. For you nonfamous plebes, this refers to any time you're running the show—parties in your honor, social events you're hosting, that kind of thing.

You're winging for a fellow betch: The point of winging is not to sit there and barely tolerate it as your friend chats up guys, but to actually complement her in doing so. Sitting there rolling your eyes while your friend and the guy she just did a shot with suck face doesn't make you a good wing-betch, it makes you a particularly burdensome accessory. Take a cue from guys and "jump on the grenade"—that is, chat up his friend and try to have fun. You never know what might happen.

Obviously, all of these situations involve you being the one to initiate conversation, not jump in his lap. From there, it's still up to him to prove his worth. Don't freak out if you take a chance once in a while and it doesn't work out (e.g., he's not feeling it, has a girlfriend, you're actually a giant anthropomorphic sea cucumber, etc.). Even the best hitters strike out about 70 percent of the time.

Dealbreakers for Guys

What the shit? You just finished the chapter where you learn where you *might* meet guys, and you're worrying about "dealbreakers"? Tell me, are you also the kind of person who's so uptight that you make a "grilled cheese" in the microwave because your schedule is so jam-packed? You should lighten up. But fine, here are some things, I guess, that could be considered "dealbreakers" by the men you haven't even met yet.

Don't:

- Wear socks with sandals.

- Have the Miley Cyrus haircut.

- Be obviously and outwardly way too into soccer (if you're from anywhere other than the United States, replace "soccer" with "baseball").

- Smell like Tabasco sauce.

- Be Miley Cyrus.

- Burp the alphabet in public.*

- Wear a shirt with any iteration of "Keep Calm and [Verb] On."

- Be the guy's sister.**

- Sing any of the following at karaoke: "Baby Got Back," "Total Eclipse of the Heart," "Bohemian Rhapsody."

- Publicly proclaim that Taylor Swift "really gets me." (We know she does, calm down.)

- Flirt at a wedding at which you are the bride.***

---

* *Does not apply if you're under age twelve.*
** *Does not apply in . . . nope, not gonna do it. Too easy.*
*** *Negotiable.*

Dear Betches,

So here is my dilemma. I just got back from a two-week vacation in Paris for a cousin's wedding and general drinking/shopping. During one of my last nights there, I met a strapping young lad at a local pub. He'd been living in Paris for a couple months on some sort of sabbatical for his job. Wasn't really paying attention, I literally got lost in his eyes. His mouth was moving, but all I was thinking about was how he would look naked in my bed. Safe to say, we got along swimmingly, he is actually *Il est adorable* (see what I did there?). So, we are a couple drinks in and well into a deep flirty conversation about past relationships when my aunt spots us and heads over. (She's not like, a regular aunt, she's a cool aunt.) First thing she says? "Oh lovely! You guys have met! You know you're second cousins, right?"

PLOT TWIST!!!!!!!!!!!!!! I heard a huge screeching halt sound in my head. What in the actual fuck? As I'm sure you can imagine, it totally killed our vibe, and we couldn't really look each other in the eye after that. Anyway here is my question. He added me on Facebook and we have been chatting here and there. Definitely holding back, but still sort of flirting. Is it nasty that I still want to hook up with him despite the fact that we basically share the same blood? Because like, there's your cousins . . . and then there's your first cousins . . . wait that's not right, is it . . . ?

HELP ME. HE'S SO HOT. WHAT DO I DO?!?

Sincerely,
Kissing Cousins

Dear Kissing Cousins,

I'm going to ignore your annoying *il est adorable* statement and just chalk it up to you being slightly nuts, which you'd have to be if you're really considering pursuing a relationship with your cousin. Now, it's not even like you're in the territory of fourth or fifth cousins where you have no idea how you're even related, second cousins are very simple to understand. They're the children of your parents' cousins. It's fucking creepy. Plus, this guy lives in Paris. Are you telling me that the dating pool where you live is so small that you're actually considering entering a long distance relationship with a person with whom you would probably wind up producing special needs children? What are you going to tell your kids? That mommy and daddy have the same great-grandparents because, well, blah blah blah Habsburg princes did it blah blah? No. Just no.

It's fine to think your second cousin is hot, but just stay away from that shit. Aside from the creepy aspect of sharing the same bloodline, do you want to get into something with someone who's going to be at every family function for the rest of your life after you inevitably stop hooking up/hanging out/ discussing the fact that you share the same ancestry? This isn't fucking *Game of Thrones.* If you're looking to meet guys, take up a new hobby or hit the bars, not your goddamn family reunion.

Sincerely,
The Betches

SPARK NOTES

Once you feel good about yourself, it's time to get out there and meet new people who can actually enjoy those thighs you spent the last six months sculpting in barre class.

Here are some take-home points from this chapter that you should remember before embarking on the agonizing yet sometimes amazing world of dating.

- Your goal when going out should never be to meet a guy. It should be to have fun with your friends. No one likes a girl who seems like she's trying to get fucked.

- It's much easier to meet a quality guy in person when you're not blacked out. If you can't have a few drinks without losing your right contact lens and left shoe, try meeting guys through some sober activities that you enjoy.

- Give online dating a try. It opens you up a shit-ton of more possibilities and the more people you date the more likely you are to meet someone you actually like. Math, it's like, not just for tricking Aaron Samuels into liking you.

- Know what you're getting yourself into when you choose a site or app to meet people on. Not all ways of hooking up are created equal.

- Be strategic when creating your dating profile but also don't seem like you actually give a shit. It's an art.

3

The Way It Begins Is the Way It Ends

Hookups and Fuck Ups

The best thing to remember about the start of any flirtation (online or IRL) or relationship is that the way it begins is the way it will end—if you let a guy fuck around and be wishy-washy from the start, that will set the tone for all your future dates (if you even get any, loser).

The key to solid flirtation is to be just communicative enough that you're alluring without coming off as a nasty bitch. However, don't be so talkative that he thinks he can chat with you all day without taking you on a date. You're a betch and you have shit to do, and running a pro bono text therapy service isn't on your to-do list. If a guy wants your attention, he needs to buy you dinner or at least some drinks. So how do you take it from flirting to dating?

FLIRTING IN PERSON

If you meet a guy at a bar, most of the time you should not be the one approaching him unless you're feeling especially bold and you're really in a mind-set where you don't give a shit about the possibility of him turning you down or about running the risk that he's fugly up close. Approaching guys should really only be done if the guy seems worth it, a.k.a. he's known to be shy or like, you run into Ryan Gosling at SoulCycle. So, minus those exceptions, the key, obvs, is to get the guy to approach you. There are a few things you should have locked down when you go out hoping to meet guys.

Eye Contact: This one is really fucking important as very few bros will just approach a random out of nowhere with absolutely zero sign she's into him. If you're hot enough, most of the time all it takes is a good ten-second eye-fuck to get a guy to approach you, and tbh it's really more like three seconds.

If you're staring at a guy for ten seconds without so much as an acknowledgment, what exactly is it about Ray Charles that makes him so attractive to you? If you're not looking cute you might have to rely on an intro or "accidentally" bumping into him while getting a drink. But I'd be careful with the latter because this usually doesn't happen as suavely as it does in the movies. In real life, because you're thinking about what you're about to do, you will bump into him too lightly, he won't feel it, and you'll be in a weird limbo of deciding whether you should do it again and won't realize you're awkwardly still standing next to him, mumbling to yourself. Or, because you're so concentrated on getting his attention you'll bump into him so hard that the only response you'll get is "Watch where you're going, Shrek." If you're not hot, try smiling.

Smiling: True, most betches have mastered the art of a resting bitch face, but try to make an exception when at the bars with your friends and there's a guy nearby whom you'd like to approach you. Girls who smile are more approachable. That said, there are plenty of guys who will be intrigued by your miserable face and will find a challenge in approaching the unapproachable like, "You don't look like you're having fun," or some other annoying pickup line. Avoid those men. They're not interested in you, they're just mistaking your misery for low self-esteem and figure you'll be an easy lay. Again, the uglier you are, the more important smiling will be.

There are two types of smilers in this world. The Julia Robertses and the Kristen Stewarts. Julia will smile and the entire room lights up. Kristen on the other hand will smile and it's a crapshoot. If she's genuinely happy, her smile will make her look even prettier. If she's forcing it, though, she'll look like she just realized she needs to put in a tampon. Know which you are. If you're a KStew, smiling at guys across a room is almost always unnatural and awkward. So here's a super-useful tip: Stop ignoring everything your friend is saying for just a minute and engage, genuinely laugh at what they say and then, as your laugh transitions into a smile, glance over at the guy and stay on him for two seconds. When you feel your fake happiness start to fade, immediately look away and continue as you were, fake listening to your bestie.

Three Besties or Less Rule: If you're going out with a ginormous fucking gaggle of girls and you're all huddled in the corner, no guy is going to approach any of you. Why would he risk embarrassing himself in front of twelve hot girls? It's rare that a guy has enough confidence to do this and if he does, he's most likely a huge douche lord. And if he doesn't, he's afraid that when he tries to say hello you're going to roll your eyes in his face and when he walks away, all sad and shit, your friends are all going to laugh at him in unison. I mean, who's he kidding? Less far-fetched things have happened.

If you're trying to get a guy to hit on you, chill with no more than two girls at a time and preferably just one wingwoman. No one is trying to earn the nickname "awkward bar creeper" because he got shot down in front of judgmental assholes, a.k.a. your BFFs.

The Ideal Wingbetch: The ideal wingwoman genuinely wants you to meet a guy and hopes for the best for you. She's not afraid to (privately) tell you when you're being a bitch or too fucked up to function and will tell any guy who flirts with you how amazing you are (subtly, of course, you don't want these bros to think the two of you are dating). Beware of the wingwoman who "secretly" hopes for your failure and will try to cock-block or sabotage your chances with a guy because she's jealous of you, can't help her end-less thirst for male attention, or is just selfishly trying to keep you unattached.

Good Wingbetch	Shitty Wingbetch
Introduces you to a guy you said was hot since you're shy and awkward.	Tells the guy you think is hot that you're shy and awkward.
Convinces the rest of your friends to chill at this bar for a little because you're hitting it off with someone.	Tells you everyone is leaving without you in two seconds if you don't stop talking to this guy.
Reminds you privately to smile and take your birth control.	Reminds the guy to wear a condom.
Gets herself a drink once she sees you two are getting along.	Starts talking about herself and bitching once she sees you two are getting along.

So, let's pretend that by now he's managed to success-fully single you out and get your attention long enough for a one-on-one conversation. Keep it light and talk about topics like why you're at this bar (don't say because it's cheap and you're broke AF), where he went to school (try not to cringe when his alma mater has the word "state" in it), and how cute your new necklace is (very, duh). Try and talk about positive things, as no one wants to hear you, say, talking shit about how bored you are because everyone at this bar is weird, for instance. Also, this goes without saying: Make sure you don't talk about other guys if you actually want to go out with this person. If he fucking sucks, casually mention you have a boyfriend, but if he seems chill, you should let him buy you a drink. If he doesn't offer to buy you a drink, especially if your vodka soda is mainly ice, ditch him and find a gentleman.

The power move is to talk to this guy for no more than thirty minutes, then casually tell him you're leaving to go to another bar with your friends. Don't give him too much attention or he'll think yours isn't worth much. A drunken make-out isn't a huge deal, but definitely leave it at that, and only if this is the last stop on your quest for love for the night. DO NOT fucking take any guy you just met home with you. Ideally your first encounter gets him intrigued, but as a rule of thumb you should exit at the crescendo of your conversation and always leave him wanting more. If he wants to see you again he will ask for your number, and the games will begin. (If he does not ask for your number, he does not want to see you again. Move along.)

Okay, so now he has your number. The need to be at the peak of your game has never been more important. Because it's 2016 and most men aren't trying to call you or show up to your door to ask you out in person, most of this shit is annoyingly done through text. It's okay, though, because as you'll see this has its advantages and disadvantages.

Inspirational Hard-to-Get Betch: Cinderella

Cinderella was really poor and she like, didn't get out much. Scrubbing floors is not betchy but when she finally got a makeover by her ~~stylist~~ Fairy Godmother she made sure to take the opportunity to get blackout and go to the biggest singles event of the season. It only took one night out for her to meet Prince Charming, which is kind of a misnomer because after all, it was *her* elusive charm that had him hooked. She gave the prince a couple of dances, got wasted and lost her shoe, then peaced-out without even saying good-bye. This was a truly betchy move, and she had the prince so obsessed with finding her that he toured the kingdom just to return her fucking shoe. **Moral of the story:** Be elusive, and he will think you're worth chasing.

FLIRTING VIA TEXT

For betches, the dating world can be a scary place. From creepy guys who seem normal at first to funny guys who are secretly poor, it's sometimes hard to spot the keepers among the unfaithful Wall Street pros on this journey of love and not doing work. But even scarier than the prospect of contracting HPV—not scary anymore, there's a vaccine—is the potential for the silent relationship killer: Awkward Texting Dynamic (ATD).

The bro with ATD might even be normal in person,

but after less than a week of talking to him via the written word you realize he's *useless* as a texter. This will inevitably become a dealbreaker as he's managed to fuck up your chief form of communication. Honestly, in many cases we'd prefer a guy have a crooked dick than consistently use the wrong form of "you're" in conversation. Let's break down the ways that a guy can ruin his prospects with you via his ATD.

Too Sarcastic for Real Conversation

In an attempt by both of you to show off how clever and insightful you are, you are trying to one-up each other with sarcastic comments as varied in subject matter as the reasons why Ibiza is really overrated. Eventually the need to consistently one-up each other leads to such an intense breakdown of the conversation that you have no clue what the fuck this guy is even talking about.

> **Him:** *Well I'd meet you at that bar but I'm pretty sure they won't let in people with as amazing a haircut as mine.*
>
> **You:** *Haha well you can try giving the bouncer one of your famous hugs.*
>
> **Him:** *But really, should we put all our eggs in one basket?*

At this point, no one knows what is going on. Is this bro coming to meet you or not? Should you answer this weird text or hope he follows up clarifying what his actual plan is? Too much sarcasm spoils the broth.

Does He Hate You or Is He Trying to Be Funny

This happens when a guy responds so awkwardly to a seemingly easy enough text that you're not sure whether he doesn't give a shit or he's just making a bad joke.

> **You:** *Kk have a good night*
>
> **Him:** *Haha "good"*

Now you're thinking like, what the fuck does THAT mean. Fucking asshole. This weirdness almost forces you to ask him to clarify, which under normal circumstances you'd never actually do. Or, you can play the higher card and simply ignore. We vote for the latter, obviously. Either way, wondering if a guy thinks you're a joke does not improve your chances of living happily ever after.

Sarcasm Mismatch

As a betch, you're one of the smartest, quickest people in the world. You have the perfect comeback in under ten seconds and your wit is on par with Tina Fey's. Unfortunately, much of the population, including potential bros you may encounter, might not be the brightest candles on the cake.

> **You:** *Good thing I always wake up early on Sundays after drinking.*
>
> **Him:** *Haha really? Usually I sleep forever!*

At this point you're not sure if you should just go with it or do the even more awkward thing and clarify what you're talking about. One thing's for sure, if he can't get your snarky mean-spirited texts he'll never get you. End it now.

The Drifter Who Floats In and Out of Consistently Texting You

This guy has been up your ass about asking how your day is going and what you got your mom for Mother's Day for like, forty-eight hours straight. Then suddenly, after asking you what your plans are for Blackout Wednesday he drops off the face of the fucking planet. You've just about written this guy off as dead to you when out of nowhere you get a "Happy Friday!" text at noon two days later. Where the fuck have you been, bro? And what kind of text is *Happy Friday*? My aunt texts me that.

The Bad Speller

This one is pretty self-explanatory. The guy seemed smart enough when you met him. I mean, he said he went to Penn! Unfortunately he's as good of a speller as Kendall Jenner after fifteen tequila shots.

Him: *hey whatr u up 2 latr?*

Ugh, while some people can be desperate enough to write this one off as the guy being simply too cool to even give a shit about the fact that his spelling and grammar are on par with those of a first semester ESL student, true betches will write this laziness off as a dealbreaker. If you can't be bothered to write all the letters contained in the word "later" there's no shot you're going to put any thought into my birthday gift.

The Overly Friendly/Maybe Gay Texter

There are some guys who never really learned how to curb their enthusiasm in an effort to seem elusive or chilled out. This guy is one of them.

> **You:** *How's your Saturday going? Still hungover?*
>
> **Him:** *Nope! Just walking my dog around the park! He loves playing with the other puppies! So excited for the game later!!!!!*

This guy is more enthused about his upcoming Saturday dentist appointment than a Make-A-Wish kid at Disney World. His overexcitement to see you is nothing short of uncomfortable. Chill the fuck out, bro, I can guarantee your dog taking a shit is not that exciting. If I wanted to hang out with an overeager twelve-year-old girl, I'd go to a One Direction concert.

The Busy Texter/Potentially Huge Asshole

The opposite of the Overly Friendly texter is the bro who's too cool for school. On the one hand, you're impressed that this bro has cooler things to do than try to see you at your earliest possible convenience, but on the other hand he might be just too lazy to be worth your time. This is the guy who asks you to hang out with two hours' notice and treats making plans as casually as brushing his teeth. Like, put some effort in if you want to see me, asshole. This is a date with ME you're planning, not lunch at The Cheesecake Factory; one more cancellation and you're dunzo.

Texting is an art and if a bro sucks at it, it will be a sign of huge frustrations for months to come. Hugh Hefner had fifteen girlfriends for a reason, and that reason is probably that he's too old to use a fucking iPhone.

A guy's early texting style will tell you a ton about his intentions with you. The time of day, details, and frequency with which he texts are all pretty correlational to how into you he is, so pay attention.

If you're wondering how often you should text him in the beginning a general rule of thumb is "the less the better." However, if you're never going to text him first, your text responses to him should be enthusiastic *or*

> *"Never make someone a priority when all you are to them is an option."*
> —Maya Angelou

somewhat long (key: somewhat, leave the essays for your English professor). If you want to text him, then figure that for every two times he texts you first you can text him first, but only with something funny/interesting to say. Like, don't ask him how his day went. Not only should you not really care yet, but this will make him think you're thinking about him randomly and makes the chase that much less exciting.

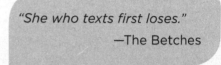

"She who texts first loses."
—The Betches

Don't be offended if a guy's texts indicate he just wants to have sex. That's his prerogative, but it doesn't mean you have to put up with that shit if you're looking for something more. If you want a relationship and he wants to fuck around, you should end things immediately and not waste your time. Here's how to tell if a bro is into you in those very early dating stages or if he's just trying to get it in.

He's Trying to Date vs. He's Just Trying to Get Laid

He's Trying to Date If He . . .	He's Just Trying to Fuck If He . . .
Sends you Snapchats of his dog.	Sends you Snapchats of his dick.
He likes and comments on your Instagrams.	He likes and comments on Jen Selter's Instagrams.
He asks you for plans with more than twenty-four hours' notice.	He asks you for plans with less than twenty-four minutes' notice.
He compliments your mom's cooking.	He compliments your mom's ass.
You're stressed out about work and he texts you to say good luck.	You're stressed out at work and he texts you to say he might have herpes.
Tells you he likes a girl who likes an occasional night in.	Tells you he likes a girl who likes an occasional dick in her ass.

What Would Karen Do?

When texting, Karen texts long-as-fuck paragraphs and constantly asks questions even when none are asked of her. She overanalyzes every single thing a guy says and is always the first one to initiate a conversation and the last one to speak in it. After two dates she'll text a guy that she misses him and can't wait to hang out again. She is a certified stage-5 clinger. In short, she is every guy's worst nightmare because they can't get rid of her no matter how much they ignore her, as she will take even the slightest polite response to indicate that he is really into her and will continue to text him despite his clear lack of pursuit of her.

FLIRTING VIA SOCIAL MEDIA: HOW TO MAKE SURE YOU NEVER GET A DICK PIC

Flirting on social media versus IRL is very different. Here's an easy guide to follow on the apps of our choice.

Facebook

Do:

- Accept his friend request.
- Let him comment on your pictures.
- Like his pictures *occasionally.*

- Put your Instagrams on Facebook if he doesn't follow you on Insta, with geotags if you're somewhere cool.

Don't:

- Chat him.

- Friend his friends.

- Like all of his pictures.

- Like any of his friends' pictures.

- Like any picture older than one month.

Twitter

Who the fuck flirts on Twitter anymore? What are you going to do, write him a haiku?

Snapchat

Do:

- Add him (if he has followed or friended you already or if he told you to add him).

- Send him pics of what you're doing, like walking your dog, or drinking outside with your friends.

- Send him pics of something that was very obviously a joke between you two.

- Make your story really hot/super-fun pics of you and your friends.

Don't:

- Send him pics of your sweaty face right after the gym.

- Send him pics of your boobs and/or naked body.

- Send him a pic first more than once a week.

- Make your story really gross/super-fun videos of you popping your pimple.

Instagram

Do:

- Follow him back.

- Like some of his pictures.

- Put up pics of you in a bathing suit but not looking thirsty.

Don't:

- Like his pictures from thirty weeks ago.

- Comment on pictures unless he's done so first.

- Accidentally like his ex-girlfriend's pic.

If a guy's early texting or social media dynamic points to the fact that he's just looking to fuck around, then we promise he's just looking to fuck around. Guys will not notice what a cool girl you are and suddenly decide they're ready for a relationship. It might happen once in a blue moon, but looking for a relationship that way is like driving your car into walls until you find one that won't damage it. That wall may exist, but you're going to do a lot of damage trying to find it. You cannot change him into someone who is ready for a relationship and who wants to date you. Not everyone is going to love you, and you need to get over that because you have no control over it.

What you do have control over is the amount of nonsense you put up with and the amount of respect you command. If someone is treating you like they don't give a shit, it's because they don't give a shit. Figure out what he wants (meaning: pay attention) and if you don't want the same thing, you need to bounce faster than Rob Kardashian from a mirror. Think of it this way: You are Harvard. Some people (not many, but some) turn down Harvard, so it's not the end of the world when a guy for some reason feels he'd rather go to Yale.

> *"If someone shows you who they really are, believe them."*
> —Maya Angelou

Flirting: From a Bro's Perspective
by Head Pro

Men don't do themselves a lot of favors when it comes to dating, particularly not in the instance of flirting. To understand why men are so goddamn inept at something as simple as walking up and saying "hi," you have to understand two things:

1. Men are under the impression that you've got it easy. That is, we have to do all of the asking and the woman is able to just sit back and soak it all in. Most men don't know what it's like to be cornered by someone who makes you uncomfortable or afraid, or even to be stuck in a conversation with someone who just won't. Fucking. Go. Away. So, we figure the hard part is up to us, and if a person convinces himself that something's going to be difficult, odds are he's probably going to suck at it.

2. Every man's deepest fear is emasculation. Sure, the threat pales in comparison to the violence and intimidation women fear from men, but whatever, it's real. This is why the most common flirting advice for men from women ("forget the pickup lines and just introduce yourself!") falls on deaf ears: Being yourself means putting your actual self out there, and men are terrified of vulnerability. If he goes up to a girl and says, "Hi, I'm Jake, what's up?" and gets rejected, it's devastating. Because Jake went in there with nothing to hide behind—no pickup line to scoff at, no drink to decline—all there was for her to reject was him. That is fucking *brutal* for our fragile egos.

So what can you do to ease a dude's anxiety?

Go Out With a Game Plan

Proper planning prevents piss-poor pickup lines, as they say. If you're going out with friends, determine beforehand who's looking to meet guys, or is at least open to the idea. Nothing's going to throw a guy off his game like Becky's drunk ass waddling up and being all *[Hiccup] Who the fuck are you and why do you think you can talk to my friend?* It puts guys on the defensive and is embarrassing. Besides, just use girl magic to call in the troops if a guy's company is unwanted.

Show That You're Having Fun

It's not your obligation to be the life of the party, but if you're having fun where you are, show it—smile, laugh, dance, etc. The kind of guys you'd want to talk to (that is, guys who are chill and social and having fun) look for the same things in girls.

Make Eye Contact

Like the Betches said, easily the biggest thing you can do to ease the transition from "ooh, she's hot" to "hey gorgeous, what's your name," and it costs you practically nothing. When a guy feels like you want his attention, his stress level drops about 1,000 percent, and he's *way* less likely to hide behind lame come-ons. Throw a smile in there if you're not sure he's picking up what you're laying down, and it'll be smooth sailing (if he's interested, that is).

Don't Be Afraid to Break the Ice

I'm aware this borderline violates some tenet of betchiness, but I'm not talking about outright hitting on a guy. If a guy you have your eye on (and who you suspect has his eye on you) isn't taking the bait, consider a harmless non sequitur to break that invisible barrier.

THE FATEFUL FIRST DATE

No relationship (postcollege) could exist without a first date. Whether you met through a friend, at a bar, or through Instagram comments, you two will exchange numbers and make plans to get to know each other further. But that's where things get murky. How does he ask you out? Where does he take you? What do you wear? What if he wears Crocs? Don't cry sad, sad girl, we're here to help.

Dating in College

For the vast majority of people in college, dating is like, not a thing. Dating is about getting to know one another and when you're in school, the bubble is usually so small that you already knew almost everything there was to know about this guy. It's the nature of Greek life and the rumor mill. You guys will usually meet at a frat party and then hang out and hook up for so long that it's just sort of assumed you're "dating."

The college equivalent of dating is something along the lines of him charging your hangover Seamless breakfast to his dad's credit card after a themed mixer. You'll know you're dating in college when everyone in your sorority house knows his name and how he likes his breakfast made by the house chef because he's there every fucking morning.

Assuming there's no awkward texting dynamic and the bro promptly asks you when you're free for a date, you should never accept the first day he suggests unless that's literally the only time you can swing. Remember, you're busy as fuck. Just because what you're busy with is an ABC Family Movie marathon is no reason to accept the first date he proposes. He doesn't need to know what you're doing, only that you're in demand. So, suggest a different day and if he can't do that then agree to the next one he suggests.

> "What is it with the weekends now? I swear to God every guy I've fucked since Memorial Day wants to know what I'm doing this weekend. They just don't get it. My weekends are for meeting new guys so I don't have to keep fucking the old ones."
>
> —Samantha, *Sex and the City*

Make it work but don't be so amenable that you appear desperate for male interaction. That's what Tinder is for.

The first few dates should try to be scheduled for weekdays because you have a shit-ton of other important fun stuff to do on a Friday night with your friends besides waste it meeting a guy whom you barely know for a drink. You only get two weekend nights per week. Think about who really deserves them. You'll know you really give a fuck about a guy when you're actually willing to forgo your bestie's thousandth Saturday night pregame to let him take you to dinner.

Finally, the day of your date has arrived and the worst has happened. You have no fucking idea what to wear! Take a minute to breathe. This is the moment you have been preparing for at yogalates. You can do this. Here's what you do:

1. Don't go too fancy. You don't want him to think you bought an entire new outfit for this occasion. I mean, you probably did but, again, the less he knows the better. If you're going to wear a dress or a skirt, make sure the heels are casual. Tight jeans with a tank or top that you sleep in will do. And wear something you're comfortable in so that you don't spend the entire night fidgeting, making sure the button on your top doesn't bust into his eyeball. But remember, "comfortable" never means you've fallen into the Gap.

2. Don't go too slutty. Key word here is "too." Don't wear a turtleneck, but don't wear a crop top with low-rise shorts, either. Find a chic medium that shows skin but leaves room for the imagination. The goal here is that if there's a lull in the conversation, he won't notice because he'll be wondering what your cleavage leads to. If he can basically see what your nipples look like, well, then he's probably not going to notice the lull, either, because he'll be too focused on getting rid of his boner.

3. Don't go all Kardashian Glam Squad. Never wear too much makeup on the first date. Unless he's

Helen Keller's cousin with similar vision impairment issues, he will always notice and will equate slathering it on with insecurities. Did you ever wonder why men don't watch *Real Housewives*? It's because Teresa Giudice's face looks more overdone than the phrase "sorry not sorry." Get that shit down to clear, even, bronzed skin, natural blush, with some subtle eye shadow and eyeliner, and either a trendy dark lip or a light-pink gloss. If you have serious issues and don't know how to tone it down, then we don't know what to tell you. Watch YouTube?

He Cancels Last Minute

This happens often and can be very disheartening. You have been looking forward to this date all week. You haven't eaten a single carb, not even butter. You even washed your hair. It's total bullshit. But don't let yourself be upset. If he doesn't reschedule immediately FORGET this bro. He clearly didn't care as much as you did and that's the end of that. Don't send angry texts that he'll inevitably forward to his friends. Just say *No worries maybe another time* while internally thinking he can go fuck himself and see where he takes it. Find another friend and go out with her. If there's no one to go out with, well then think of it this way: Your hair looks nice for tomorrow and you have extra calories for froyo tonight. We'll even let you get pizza this one time. Just kidding.

Now that you look fucking amazing it's time for the highly anticipated date. Everyone knows there's a lot that can go wrong on a first date, but let's just say for the sake of this example he's good looking, arrives on time, you arrive five minutes late, the place he chose has excellent lighting, and the vodka sodas are flowing. It's now up to your inter- action and chemistry to make tonight go as smoothly as possible.

How much to drink: Two drinks, min to max. You should probably have two drinks to minimize awkwardness and max- imize flirtation. No one will judge you for having two drinks, but if you're like, *Yeah keep them coming* and by the end of the night are walking around the city barefoot asking if he minds that you unhook your bra *because it's like, soooooo uncomfortable*, maybe keep two drinks as your maximum. If you guys happen to hit it off and go to another place for some more drinks, be mindful of your tolerance and suggest getting some food so that you do not drink yourself into a ditch or worse, his bed.

The Conversation: First dates shouldn't be hard for you as all you have to do is talk about yourself. Okay, fine. That's not *all* you have to do. The key is to create a balance of you and him. If he keeps asking questions then reciprocate. Keep it light. Seem interested, but don't seem like a stalker. Don't ask what his name is again or what his tax refund was last year. You can ask him things like, does he like dogs, what bars does he like, what are his favorite movies, blah blah blah. And please, don't get deep into topics that you don't know shit about like the stocks he's trading or like, politics.

Shit Bat-Shit-Crazy Bitches Do:
Reveal Too Much Information on a First Date

You're trying to remain a little mysterious here, so one of the worst things you can do is reveal too much personal information on a first date. It's fine to reveal surface level shit like the fact that you love movies and hate carbs, but don't be the maniac who brings up her seventh-grade eating disorder or delves into the reasons for her most recent breakup. No one wants to hear about that shit.

First dates are about pretending to be normal for long enough to get to a second date, where you also continue to pretend to be normal until it eventually slips what a psychopath you are. This isn't a therapy session, don't reveal how you're looking for a guy that is just like your dad or that you are going to cut yourself if one more of your friends gets engaged. Being somewhat aloof on a first date will make the guy want to learn more about you as opposed to feeling like he's gotten your complete life story topped with an invitation to be the next piece of luggage on your emotional baggage carousel.

How to Act: Be flirtatious and maintain eye contact. Remember, you're on a date, not a business meeting. If you're not a naturally personable human, then pretend like you're on *The Bachelor* and "open up" or "let your guard down" or some shit like that. And if you're not Zooey-Deschanel-endearing-awkward and like, just fucking plain awkward, we suggest drinking *a little* more. That usually keeps you from looking at everything but the guy sitting across from you and knocking almost everything off the dinner table. If you're at a bar, don't look at the TV with the game on and don't underestimate the power of a subtle arm-touch.

The Check: You should never visibly expect him to pay. That's plain rude. If the date went well, every betch should do the Courtesy Fumble. Fumble through your bag for your wallet until he says something about not letting you pay. Give him some time to say, "What are you doing? Please, I got this." You should then proceed with "Oh, thanks so much!" and that'll be the end of the awkward bill discussion. ALWAYS *offer*, as in like, every time. It'll show you have class and aren't Courtney Stodden.

The Courtesy Fumble is all about the gesture, but nothing more. If he lets you take your card out and put it on the table, don't fight him about it (unless you have no money in your account, in which case you shouldn't even offer, you broke biatch). He clearly is a cheap bastard and isn't interested in impressing you at all. If he doesn't realize what a Courtesy Fumble is and actually lets you pay on a first date you need to dump his ass. Be cordial and then proceed to never answer his calls ever again.

> *"I don't want no scrubs."*
> —TLC

Guys love to be like, *but, feminism!* But we're like, *but, courtship . . . romance . . . chivalry . . . etc.* If the guy doesn't want to pay for the woman at least on a first date, he doesn't value romance or care about impressing you. Sure we're empowered as fuck and could pay for our own drinks if we want to. That doesn't mean we don't want to be treated like the queens that we are. No guy worth his weight in boat shoes is going to expect you to split the bill until at least the fourth date.

Ending the date: The date isn't officially over until you two are not physically together anymore, so there's a lot that can happen between the check and the hug and/or kiss good-bye. Maybe you guys go to a couple more places, maybe you walk around, maybe you leave it there and you go get fucked up with your friends. All that is obviously great, but the most important takeaway here is to leave the date while it's still going strong. You want him to want to see more of you, not feel like he's already seen enough. Say something like "I had so much fun tonight but have to go home because I have early brunch with my fam tomorrow." This makes you seem cute because you're a family girl and like brunch. Also, you're ending the date leaving him wanting more. Bottom line: Say no to drinks on his apartment roof deck. The only way that shit will end is you sneaking out of his apartment with makeup all over your face, unable to find the Uber app on your phone because you're so hungover, and wishing you had left more to the imagination.

   If the good-bye leads to a kiss then don't resist if you're into him. If you're not into him, avoid the awkwardness of him going for it by moving your face pretty far to the left and preemptively going in for a hug. Just don't turn this into a handshake or back pat. God help you if you're that awkward. If you like him, definitely go for it. With a few drinks in you, a kiss can give you a good sense of how this guy is in bed. If he's super smooth, then hope he thought you were the same. If he's about as spastic as someone on bath salts, well, run the fuck home. The date is over.

USE IT OR LOSE IT: DITCHING THE DEAD WEIGHT

If you and/or the person you are dating don't feel amazing about each other in the early stages, it's best to cut the cord as soon as possible. Blogger Mark Manson's Fuck Yes theory posits, "If you're in the grey area to begin with, you've already lost." The Fuck Yes theory is the idea that if you or the person you are dating don't each feel like "fuck yes," then you're both wasting your time. While we believe dating is a little more complicated than that, the general theory holds true. If you've been going around in circles trying to figure out if a guy likes you for more than three weeks it's not fucking worth it. When you're going to enter a relationship it's pretty clear very early on if two people are really into each other. Sure, playing it cool is encouraged and necessary in the beginning, but after a small cautionary period, if someone isn't really into you they're never going to be.

Signs You're in "Fuck Yes" Mode	Signs You're Feeling Meh
You can't wait to have sex with him.	You're trying to figure out just how long you can hold out before you're morally obligated to fuck him.
You're rearranging your schedule so you can see him.	You're secretly happy that something came up and you have to reschedule your third date.
You're googling clever things about your shared interests to text him.	You literally forgot he existed until he texted to ask you out again.
You can't wait for when it's socially acceptable to introduce him to your friends.	You're avoiding introducing him to anyone because you're not sure if they'll think he's weird.
His request to follow you on Instagram has you triple checking your pics to make sure you come off well.	You cringe at how awful he looks in the goofy selfie he took last weekend.

This is something to consider when you take that third date with a guy you're not that into because he's great on paper. Or if you're debating whether it's worth texting a dude you've been on four dates with because it's been a week and he hasn't contacted you. When shit is going to work out, there's excitement in the air and both people can feel it's going somewhere. Don't date bros you're lukewarm about, because the next thing you know you're settling and you have a back-burner boyfriend that you are obligated to babysit at pregames and your sister's wedding. Because you're a betch who has a ton of stuff going on and are constantly having fun and enjoying your life, you're not going to settle for a guy who makes you "Larry David at a second cousin's bris"–level enthused. Your time is super valuable, so don't waste it with a guy you think is just okay.

If someone isn't feeling "Fuck Yes" about you, ditch him. It's his loss and your time would be better spent overanalyzing the actions of a guy who is actually rightfully obsessed with you. You'll only be into one bro until the next one comes along, and when you're both in "fuck yes" mode, you'll know something legit has just happened.

A Note on Friend Integration

Again, your very full life, which includes your friends and family, should be your first priority right now. Just because you're carving out some time to go on dates does not mean you should ever ditch plans or a friend for some cute guy who asked you out. When your life is a priority, a guy is more attracted to you and the right guy won't mind waiting until next week because you have a potluck with your besties. Don't be the girl who ditches established plans for a second date. You would be pissed if a friend prioritized a guy she barely knew over you, so make sure you show your BFFs the same respect. You have a life and if you don't, get one.

PSA: DO NOT ACCEPT THESE DATES

When a guy asks you out on a date and follows through with it (i.e., he texts you a few days ahead to plan it, chooses a place and time, and doesn't cancel), betches typically won't tell him his choice sucks and pick a new one. No, we respect the bro's effort because the effort is the most important factor (at first). However, there are a large percentage of guys who put minimal effort into first dates, which is marginally understandable but definitely unacceptable.

Here is the official guide to the dates you should accept and the ones for which you suddenly come down with Ebola.

Do Not Accept: Dates 1 or 2

Guy says: "Let's walk around and find a place."

Unless he's your long-time boyfriend where this actually could be sort of fun, this means he's lazy AF. He doesn't care enough about you to do any research, a.k.a. typing a neighborhood into Yelp. Like, have some common sense, dude, we're going to wear heels, why would we want to "walk around." This would be more enticing if the offer were to "drive around in an Uber and find a place" but he wouldn't ever offer that because he's probably cheap, too.

Betch should say: Always blame it on the weather. If it's nice weather: "Do you mind picking somewhere to meet? Let's walk around after, it's gonna be so nice out." Or, "Ah

I think it's supposed to rain, do you mind picking some-where?" Or, "I'm not really feeling that well, sorry, rain check?"

Guy says: "Want to come over and _____?"

Whether *blank* is *watch a movie, cook,* or *smoke weed,* if this is your first or second date, do not accept. Few relation-ships start so close to the bedroom and the guy you're dating is no exception. While a lot of girls will think it's hard to say no to this because they're afraid to come off as "not chill" it's important to remember that unless he's an actual chef and actually wants to impress you, all he wants is to fuck. Which is fine, but like, not yet. The longer you make him wait the more he will think you are worth it.

Betch should say: "Haha oooh that sounds awesome, but I'm in the mood to go out somewhere tonight." Easy as that. If he still insists, then either stop answering his texts or take the straight-up route and say, "Honestly, I don't really know you well enough to come over just yet. Sorry!"

Do Not Accept: Dates 3 or After

Guy Says: "Want to grab drinks this Tuesday around nine p.m.?"

If a guy still hasn't taken you out to dinner, you have a problem. He's either cheap, broke, manorexic, is fucking dating-clueless, or worse, isn't taking you or this seriously. Taking a girl for drinks makes sense for dates 1 and 2. Maybe he suggests you guys order appetizers for the second one. The point is, the more time the guy wants to spend with you the more he likes you. Drinks are a 20-minute commitment to getting you drunk enough to make out while dinner is a 1.5-hour commitment to feeding your wispy, thinspo frame. He knows this, you know this, your waiter who keeps asking if you guys want to order something or still need a minute knows this. So, what's it mean if he only wants to get drinks with you each time? He's either making you think you guys are dating so you sleep with him on the third or he's just pregaming before going out. Either way, shut that shit down.

Betch Should Say: "I'm actually trying not to drink that much this week but I'd be down to grab dinner instead." If he insists on getting drinks because he has dinner plans before or some other bullshit reason you can just reply with "okay maybe some other time!" If he continues asking you for drinks keep using the same excuse. If he really wants to see you he'll take you to dinner, if not, move on and drink a bottle of wine on your couch with your roommate and watch HBO. There's no shortage of drinking buddies in your life, and your friend isn't going to bore you by talking about CrossFit.

Dear Guys Who Invite Me Over to "Watch a Movie"

Between Uber being banned in the Hamptons, the additional months I have to wait until Scandal *comes back, and the fact that* 1989 *still isn't available on Spotify, there is a lot to hate in life right now. That said, there is still nothing I hate more than when a guy I don't really know that well asks me if I want to "come over and watch a movie."*

If you're just going for the V, you need to at least put some effort in. Take me out for drinks and dinner before you invite me to your place. I can't claim that my game is on some Beyoncé-level shit, but I have a fully functioning and disease-free vagina thank you very much, and I'm counting on some work being put in on your end before I inevitably refuse to give it up. If twelve-year-olds are willing to run around an obstacle course, answer riddles from a talking tree, and embarrass themselves on live TV just to fail at putting together the Shrine of the Silver Monkey, you can expend some energy into attempting to get in my ironclad pants.

My point is: People have been willing to do a lot more for a lot less.

Shit, now that Blockbuster's gone out of business, you don't even need to leave your house to drive to the fucking store to pick up a movie. YOU DON'T EVEN NEED A PHYSICAL COPY OF THE MOVIE IN THE FIRST PLACE. Now any asshole with a working laptop and an Internet connection and his friend's brother's roommate's Netflix subscription thinks he can hit it? No, and no.

And don't think for one second I'm deluded into the whole "I'm being a nice guy who just wants to watch a movie in the company of a girl I like and incidentally also want to bone" bullshit that you might be going for. First off, if I wanted to spend time with a nice guy, I would stay home and watch something that Topher Grace is in. Second, maybe some other basic bitch would believe that you could actually get to know a person while you're sitting side by side, not looking at or talking to one another for 1.5–3 hours in front of your TV or MacBook Pro, but my four years of college partying have left me with enough functioning brain cells for common sense. So no, I'm not falling for that shit, either. . . .

Next time, I'm going to insist we watch 12 Years a Slave *and fuck your whole plan up.*

You're not as smooth as you think,
The Betches

Red Flags vs. Dating Dealbreakers

Red Flag	Dealbreaker
He doesn't make a reservation.	He makes a reservation at Señor Frog's.
He talks about the Kardashians.	He talks about Kim's style.
He wears nontrendy sneakers, Crocs, those weird shoes that are like socks with holes for your toes.	He's wearing the slightest bit of makeup.
He won't stop talking about himself.	He won't stop talking about his mom or ex-girlfriend.
He lets you split after you Courtesy Fumble.	He lets you pay for the whole thing at any point ever besides his birthday.
He orders a cosmo.	He orders a virgin piña colada.
He checks out the waitress.	He hits on the waitress.
He talks about how hot Farrah Abraham is.	He talks sexually about literally any girl besides you.
He leaves a weak tip.	He leaves no tip.

Dates 2 to 6: Keep Doing What You're Doing

Making it to the second date is probably one of the most pivotal moments in a relationship. If a guy asks you on a second date, it means your first impression was good and now you can work on not fucking up while slowly revealing more about who you really are. Getting a second date does *not* mean you should celebrate this milestone by giving head or wearing a formal dress the second time around.

The important thing is to proceed slowly and be chill. Don't try to rush the relationship or get caught up in the guy. As in, you can casually let it slip on date three that your parents are divorced but don't have a traumatic meltdown as you reveal that your mom never played Barbie enough with you as a child. Most guys have a mild to severe fear of commitment or intimacy so you should follow in his footsteps in terms of opening up about yourself. The beginning stages are all about having fun and getting to know each other, not laying all your baggage and ultimatums on the line.

If you're asked on a second date, you guys have piqued each other's interest. In addition to keeping it light, you should be taking this time to judge him to see if the two of you get along well, share similar interests, or if his profession that his "mom is a saint" is just something you cannot deal with. Once you've mastered the first date, it's all easy street from there, assuming you don't do anything psychotic like have a breakdown, get wildly drunk, or order Buffalo wings.

Dear Head Pro,

Since you are a pro, I was hoping you could have the answer to my question about the guys of our generation.

There have been two different times when I've hung out with a guy thinking that we were just hanging out and then later, after the fact, they will refer to it as "our first date" and I was unaware of the "fact" I was on a "date" with these guys at the time. And after talking with my friend, she's told me that a similar situation has happened with her several times with different guys.

I guess what I'm asking is:

1. Am I being an oblivious idiot for not realizing I'm supposed to be on "dates" with these guys or is there something wrong with these guys for being delusional daters and thinking that we were on a "date"?

2. Are my friend and I correct in assuming that for something to be a legitimate date both parties should be informed BEFORE and not after that it is a date? And if so is it the guy's responsibility to make that clear or our responsibility to ask?

3. How can I know in the future if I am on/have been on a "date" with someone before he labels it as such?

Please use your wisdom to help this betch out, Head Pro.

Confused kisses,
Betch who goes on ambiguous "dates"

_____

Dear Betch who goes on ambiguous "dates,"

This is a pretty common complaint, so much so that there's some scientific basis in it. A 2012 study called "The Misperception of Sexual Interest" found that, in general, men tend to overestimate women's interest in them, while women tend to underestimate a man's interest. This makes some sense, given the way we go about dating and courtship: Men are generally the initiators, so there's an evolutionary advantage in using your belief that every woman wants to fuck you as motivation to get up in the mix. Since women are the ones who do the choosing, it behooves you to be more selective and to assume a guy's not into you until he proves otherwise. This was probably very useful when we were hunting and gathering on the fucking Serengeti, but in modern times it leads to the kind of wacky hijinks you and your friend encounter.

That said, I'm not sure what you'd have guys do. When a guy asks you out on a romantic date, should he present you with a notarized letter of intent? Do you want some kind of dating punch card, so you know exactly the point at which you're going steady (and eligible for a free Subway foot-long)? Should they start wearing fedoras, kissing you on the hand and calling you "m'lady"? Maybe an arranged marriage would be more your style. If you're hot enough, your family could get away with as little as three goats and a barrel of soybeans for a dowry, which is a steal these days.

If none of that sounds particularly good to you, then do what most postpubescent girls do and assume that if a guy you aren't related to asks you to hang out one-on-one, it's because he's interested romantically. He doesn't (or shouldn't) have to clarify what it is—that's what he's doing when he asked you out. As adults, we don't have notes to pass or friends to act as mediators or school dances to attend, the invitation to which signals interest. While it's always possible that a guy just wants to hang out platonically, the more likely answer is that he's using the only means available to him to express his interest short of writing a note that says "Do you like me, y/n?"

If it's *not* a date, most guys will let you know. They'll use qualifiers—asking you to a concert might be a date, but asking you to a concert "because my buddy canceled on me and I don't want to waste the ticket" is likely not. Again, since men tend to assume that every woman wants to fuck us, we'll go out of our way to make it known when that's not our intention. If you're still unclear, just ask "Is this a date?" should be in every betch's arsenal.

Ambiguous kisses,
Head Pro

SPARK NOTES

How you present yourself to the world and your first impressions are one of the most important things to master in the dating world. If you can't get your foot in the door, you'll never even have the opportunity to get into a real relationship.

Capturing a bro's attention isn't hard, especially if you're a confident, funny betch who can master the subtle art of manipulation. The most important thing to remember is that the first few dates are all about keeping it fun and flirty and about looking hot without trying too hard. Here are the most important takeaways from this chapter.

- If you want to meet guys in person, go out in small groups of three or fewer, make subtle eye contact, and look like you're having a good time regardless of who's paying attention.

- When texting, keep it light and short. You don't have fucking time to go on about your day with a stranger you shouldn't give a shit about yet. If a guy isn't asking you out after three days of texting, drop him like the KONY 2012 movement. Keep a lookout for signs that a guy is looking for a serious relationship and not just a fuck buddy. Where he takes you on dates, his texting style, and how much effort he's putting into your meet-ups are all things to consider before mentally hiring a wedding calligrapher.

- "Netflix and chill" is not a good fucking early-stage date. Be selective about who you're giving your precious time to.

- Keep shit casual and light on the first few dates and this will lead to more dates. If there's ever a time to pretend to be "cool girl" who has a full, happy, exciting life it's on dates 1 to 6.

4

Don't Push It, Focker

The Early Stages

At this point you've been on a solid handful of dates. Enough dates that you've told your friends about him at drunk brunch but not so many that you're calling your grandma to tell her she can die happy now because her granddaughter has a shot in hell of getting married. Nothing has been defined and things are still casual. You're anxiously looking for signs from him that this is getting more serious and hope that things aren't going to fade into oblivion faster than you can say "romantic couples weekend trip."

> "What is love? Baby, don't hurt me."
> —Haddaway

The MOST important thing to remember during this phase is to keep your head in reality and not to get caught up in deranged thoughts of premature exclusivity or future plans. You are still having fun and hanging out. Here's how to not freak this guy the fuck out.

WHEN IT'S TOO EARLY TO SHOW YOUR CRAZY SIDE

As betches, we're all about keeping it real. We don't morph our personalities to date the bros we're with and we don't pretend to be someone we're not so that others will like us. That's what a nicegirl would do. However, TMI is real and can be the kiss of death for any relationship. There are certain things you should only reveal to your guy after he's fallen madly in love with your soft skin and adept drunk-snapchatting abilities.

This isn't to say that you should hide your inner crazy, but maybe wait until you're comfortably dating to have a bloody fistfight with your sister in which you're both pulling each other's hair over the fact that she stole your Equipment shirt without asking. I mean, when a fisherman wants to eat cod, does he just go stabbing the water with a large knife? No, he first places some sexy bait on the hook until the fish bites and *then* he mutilates the shit out of it. Fucking duh.

Don't Hold Back	You're Going to Scare the Shit Out of Him
That you're really particular about what you eat.	If you have a tantrum when the avocado in your salad has already started to oxidize.
That you're well groomed and enjoy manicures and blowouts.	If you reveal you're well groomed and enjoy waxing your upper lip.
That some foods make you feel kind of sick.	If you tell him about your colonoscopy revealing your celiac disease.
That your family annoys you sometimes.	If you scream at your dad on the phone because he refuses to pay your rent this month after he *promised* to help you.
That you tend to be a bit messy.	If your room looks like something out of *This Is the End*.
That you have a mild shopping addiction.	If you have thousands of dollars' worth of Louboutins, but hundreds of thousands of dollars in credit card debt.

Things Guys Do (and Continue to Do) That We Don't Want You to Know About by Head Pro

Underlying our dating culture is an odd narrative: Unrefined bachelors flounder about as single men, until they meet a woman. When that happens, his relationship with her quickly transforms him into a more cultured, civilized animal, due in large part to a healthy dose of her feminine sophistication. It's familiar, sure, but how fucking weird is that, when you think about it? There's no antithesis, no reverse, no mention of men molding women into beer-swilling philanderers. The assumption is that men are turds to be polished, helpless without a woman to clean them up. Judd Apatow has used this trope to make more money than your life is literally worth, but that doesn't make it any less bullshit.

Sure, some things change in the earliest stages of a relationship. A guy might make sure he's showered before he goes out that day, or he may start laundering his towels more than, say, never if he suspects he might have company for the evening. But other than that, there are plenty of questionable habits endemic to not only single men, but men in general. He may not make it known, but the guy you've been texting is probably still doing the following things:

Jerking Off: A lot of girls assume porn and monkey-spanking are just stopgaps guys use between periods of sexual activity.

Hardly. Sure, PornHub is there to get you through the lean times, but if you think about it, how fucking sad would it be if guys actually used masturbation as a stand-in for sex? Every guy's different, but it's safe to assume that whatever his porn habits before you met, they haven't changed just because he is (or may soon be) getting some. It's not about you; it's about us. It's entertainment, albeit very pleasurable entertainment. Fappers gonna fap, fap, fap, fap, fap. Never repeat the word "fap." Thanks.

Creeping on His Ex: Social media has made it more or less impossible to completely get away from people you've grown to know well. As such, from time to time, every guy likes to poke around Facebook, Instagram, etc., to see what she's been up to. It's human nature, and that doesn't change the moment you meet someone new. It's unreasonable to assume that the night you spent making out to "Can't Feel My Face" on the dance floor and the ensuing texts will erase her from his memory. I mean, it eventually will, but that's like, several chapters from now so let's not get ahead of ourselves.

Chatting Up Other Girls: Meeting someone you might click with is an awesome feeling, but we know just as well as you do that nothing's certain. Show me a girl who's hurt because she found out the guy she was into had like, four girls in his rotation, and I'll show you a guy who's bummed the girl he liked was just using him as a placeholder until whoever she was into came around. That's part of why, if we're out with our bros, we'll definitely engage in friendly conversation with girls even if we're feeling you. Even in a more established relationship, we'll still be polite, pleasant, and maybe even a little flirtatious if we find ourselves in that situation. It's just good social skills, if you think about it. Would you want to be with a guy who shuts down every conversational invite with "Whoa, whoa. I'm sorry, but I have a girlfriend and can't talk to you"? If you want a doormat, go to Target.

Living in Relative Filth: I don't think there's any denying that—speaking in broad terms, of course—men are more oblivious to filth than women. Part of that is because our mothers generally did all of our shit for us when we were young, whereas there's only a slight chance they imparted upon us the wisdom of, you know, actual cleanliness. It also doesn't help that we spend four-plus years in college living around a bunch of *other* guys who have no idea what clean looks like, and so by the time we graduate we're pretty desensitized to it. Even if a guy meets a girl and he can vaguely sense that he ought to tidy up, I guarantee you the sheets haven't been washed in months and that he's literally never cleaned the bathroom floor, just for instance. Fear not, we do grow out of it. Kind of.

EARLY-STAGE SOCIAL MEDIA ETIQUETTE: TAKE THE BACKSEAT

Social media has changed the relationship game forever. No longer will your ex disappear into oblivion once you break up, and no longer will you only get insights into a person's essence from simple conversation. Gone are the days when you could break up with your college boyfriend and not hear anything about him until you read his obituary in the newspaper or he showed up drunk and throwing punches at your husband at your ten-year reunion. You now have an entire identity that the world can pass judgment on in minutes and, believe us, they will.

The early stages of social media dating etiquette are pretty simple for betches. You don't follow first, you get followed.

Hopefully you'll have at least been on three dates before a guy requests you on Instagram, Facebook, Snapchat, Vine, etc., because that's long enough that he has a general sense of who you are before gaining social media access to you, i.e., before judging you solely based on that adorable picture of your new sandals that you uploaded at your beach house. If you don't like him or you don't know him that well, don't accept. He could be a dangerous stalker or, worse, a cheesy commenter. There's nothing more embarrassing than having some weirdo who comments "When am I seeing you again?" on your bikini picture, only to have to explain to your friends that it's just a guy you made out with on spring break for like, forty-five seconds. Okay, fine, it's a little flattering. But still unacceptable.

Yes, you should always follow back if you like the guy—but not immediately, you sad, desperate loser. Be aware that accepting a bro's social media requests will mean you will get constant updates about where he is, what he's doing, and whom he's with. This is a Pandora's box you may regret opening when pangs of jealousy overcome you. What girl hasn't freaked the fuck out upon seeing a picture of a guy she's seeing with his arm around another girl? You typed out a furious text only to realize that that girl is actually his cousin. Awkz.

Until you two are official, it's best to be sparing with your interaction with social media. You can like his posts if he likes yours, and you can even make a cute comment if you're feeling especially bold. Be reserved, though, because no one wants a girl who is staking claims in cyberspace on someone she doesn't actually have.

Never, we repeat, NEVER upload a picture of the two of you before you have defined what you are. It is creepy and aggressive to upload a couple's pic before you guys are a couple, and it's never the power move. It will also be awkward when and if you get ghosted and your mom is texting you asking how your new boyfriend is and telling you

"It was once said that a person's eyes are the windows to their soul. That was before people had cell phones."
—Blair Waldorf, *Gossip Girl*

that she already e-mailed the picture to your grandma, who thinks you two are going to make excellent-looking babies.

What Would Karen Do?

Karen is insane on social media. When she likes a guy, she follows him immediately even if they've never technically spoken before. She likes all of his pictures and stalks out where he went last weekend so she can be sure to frequent the same bars. She's about as subtle as herpes and she tries to assert her closeness to a guy she's hooked up with by plastering his Instagram with comments and likes. Of course, he does not comment on any of her social media and will probably make fun of how obsessed with him she is to all of his friends.

SOCIAL MEDIA: A CURSE FOR THE SHADY BROS LIVING IN A SHADY WORLD

If you happen to be dating a guy who's a bit shady (good luck with that . . .), with Instagram geotags, Facebook privacy settings, and your amazing stalking skills, no longer will he be able to get away with claiming to stay in when he's really going out; you will most definitely see the tagged pic of that bitch from his office at happy hour with him.

This is both good and bad news for you. Good because he can no longer get away with being a real life Don Draper and having dozens of side chicks while you think he just has a really late night at work. That said, some guys are easily jealous and your BF might get a little angry if he sees you on the shoulders of a random at Coachella because the view was just too good to pass up.

WHAT HIS SOCIAL MEDIA SAYS ABOUT HIM: LESS IS MORE

In general, it's kind of lame for a guy to be obsessed with social media. Sure the occasional Knicks game friend pic or Snap with his bros at a charity event is fine, but if you're with a guy who takes mirror pics, posts excessive selfies, or over-filters you'll definitely want to reconsider your relationship. Nothing is lamer than a guy who takes shirtless pics or seeks validation via social media. If your boyfriend has the social media presence of a Kardashian it probably means he's an insecure attention-seeker, self-obsessed, or a closet homo-sexual.

Generally, a guy who uses social media less will be ideal because you don't have to see what he's up to and he probably has a real life. Beware of dudes who follow excessive Instagram models and be super aware of guys who feel the need to "like" pictures of said girls. I mean, what is the point of liking an ass shot of a random Insta-whore? Does he think she's going to notice her 12,534th like and automatically fall in love with the creepy bro who's stalking her? Even worse, everyone can see these pictures and the last thing you want is all your friends asking you why the guy you're dating has a thing for size triple F fake boobs.

> *"Don't ever date a man that takes more selfies than you."*
> —Anon

Shit Crazy Bitches Do: Confront a Nonboyfriend About His Social Media Presence

If a guy is not your boyfriend, he owes you nothing. So when you confront a guy about who his new Facebook friends are or casually ask him who else he's sending Snapchats to, you just seem possessive and desperate. As we said, try not to look at his social media while you're casually dating, as nothing good can come of it. Just like nothing you do is his business, he doesn't owe you anything yet in the real world or in cyberspace. Plus, that girl you happened to see on his Instagram follower list (that you refresh daily) is probably his sister, so chill the fuck out.

Dealbreakers from a Guy's Perspective by Head Pro

The good news is that our dealbreakers, in the grand sense, aren't going to be much different than yours. The other good news is that "big picture" dealbreakers are more or less where we stop—there's no minutiae concerning what you do for a living or how our last name will pair with your first, for instance. The bad news, however, is that guys can be annoyingly fickle when it comes to why a girl just isn't doing it for us (oftentimes, we can't even articulate why). There's not shit you can do about that (and you'll go nuts trying), so focus on these big items instead:

Having Like, Obviously Horrendous Opinions: It kind of goes without saying, but if you've got some hot takes to give on subjects like The Blacks, The Jews, The Muslims, The Mexicans, etc., guys are gonna head for the hills. Basically, don't be a racist.

Being Too Tall/Short: Men have incredibly fragile egos, and unfortunately most of us directly tie our masculinity to how far we tower above our paramours. Believe it or not, I've heard guys complain that a girl was too short, too. No, I don't get it, either. It might have something to do with feeling like they're not using their height to its full advantage (i.e., not walking arm in arm with a tall, statuesque woman), maybe?

I don't know. The good thing is that guys who don't give a shit about things like this will have no qualms pursuing you. A good guy won't sweat a few inches either way and will be more than willing to climb that tower. Always keep in mind that if a guy's being shitty about your height, he's the one with the problem.

Looking Wildly Out of Touch: Guys may not have any clue what's trendy or what's stylish, but we will notice if everyone at the bar is wearing work clothes and you're chilling in jeans and a ratty T-shirt. Not a big issue for adults, typically, but I've seen some college/postgrad betches fall into this kind of lull.

Being Overly Gross/Inappropriate: It's true (and kind of shitty) that we afford men WAY more leeway when it comes to vulgarity and off-color humor. But that doesn't mean that you should stick it to The Man by telling Holocaust jokes and cussing like an eleven-year-old who just learned the word "fuck." The older people get—regardless of gender—the more boorish this makes them seem. You don't want to be that girl who giggles whenever someone says the word "butthole" (though it is pretty funny, tbh), but remember that you're having a conversation, not auditioning to be the next Howard Stern.

Discussing Religion/Politics/Money: I'd rather talk to the girl telling the Holocaust jokes. Note: This does not apply if you live in DC or NYC, where not talking ENOUGH about politics and money (respectively) counts as a dealbreaker.

So yeah, in general most of this is stuff that if you don't do it already, you don't need to worry about it. If one or more of these things apply to you, though, not only should you consider cleaning up your act for dating purposes, but maybe reevaluate your life in general while you're at it.

What Guys Think When You Decide to Have Sex with Them

For literally a century (and probably more), women have heard countless verses of the same shitty song: Don't give it up too early. Why would he buy the cow when he can get the milk for free? No one wants the ice cream truck when you're giving away the popsicles. Have sex too soon, and he won't see you as the kind of girl he can take home to mom. No one values that which is easily gotten. And on and on and on. This is problematic for a couple of reasons: For starters, it transforms sex from an activity two people (or more, if that's how you get down) *do* into a "thing" for men to obtain. This basically reduces you to a walking vagina, which is equal parts sad and anatomically impossible. They say in successful relationships and sports teams that the whole is greater than the sum of its parts; women are greater than the sum of their holes.

But there's also another, often overlooked issue: As with the tired sayings in the above paragragh, are these old sayings even true?

I'm just going to lay it out there: *A guy who doesn't text you back after you fuck wasn't going to stick around for long anyway.* Women tend to think sex flips off some kind of "commitment" switch in our minds, assuming that since you banged someone too soon, they now have no incentive to stick around. It's a classic case of confusing correlation with causation. I mean, think about it—if sex actually worked that way, would there *ever* be a "right" time to put out?

An old saying that *is* actually true is "sex won't make him love you." That is, when the guy you banged on the second date doesn't take you on a third, it's not because of the sex, it's because he probably wasn't into you enough to ask for a third date, regardless. The poor girl who can't hang on to the dudes she fucks isn't necessarily too slutty for her own good; she's just like, *really* bad at picking guys.

Of course, that's not to say that there isn't a good reason to hold back on sex for a little while. It mostly boils down to how into a guy you are, and how personally and intimately you regard sex: Ask yourself, *how much do I like this guy?* And *how devastated would I be if things fizzled out after the fourth (or whatever) date?* Now, ask yourself if you'd feel even *worse* about it if you'd also had sex in that time period. Dating outside of sex allows the two of you to get to know and evaluate each other, and ultimately become in-

"Why am I so emotional?"
—Sam Smith

vested if everything works out. Generally, people don't bail on things they're personally invested in. That's why it's called "dating" and not "finding people to fuck until you decide to get married."

Basing your decision on when to have sex on what "guys" think is kind of impossible. Lots of guys don't give a shit—your first date could involve a kilo of molly, a drum of lube, and enough condoms to fill the Mariana Trench, and you could end up married six months later! Of course, there definitely exist men who, despite actively enjoying and participating in early-term sex, have some very deep-seated personal issues that cause them to shame your quote-unquote whorishness. These men are bad people. But you won't know they're bad people unless they have it tattooed on their foreheads, so erring on the side of caution is always a good idea. Definitely don't bang him on the first date (unless you're not that into him and just want to get something out of it), but past the third or fourth date, trust your gut and do what feels right.

> "Men don't realize that if we're sleeping with them on the first date, we're probably not interested in seeing them again either."
> —Chelsea Handler

Inspirational Fictional Betch: Daenerys Targaryen

I will take what is mine with fire and blood.

Dani T. epitomizes the need to love yourself first before anyone else can give a shit about you. In season 1 of *Game of Thrones* she is a quiet, lame nicegirl who lets her brother and husband take advantage of her because she doesn't think she has any worth. With a little help from Jorah and the realization that she's a fucking queen, Dani transforms herself into a power betch who gets what she wants and manipulates everyone around her. She tells her brother to go fuck himself (i.e., has him killed), reclaims her birthright, manages to transform her husband, Drogo, from aggressive rapist into someone who is basically her errand boy, and gives birth to fucking dragon minions. By the most recent season Dani has an entire nation following her every word and pretty much every bro in the seven kingdoms wanting to fuck her. Moral of the story: By realizing that she has had the power all along within herself, Dani managed to propel her self-love into the love and admiration of everyone around her.

SERIOUSLY, THOUGH: DON'T FUCKING GET AHEAD OF YOURSELF

You are both still in the "getting to know each other" stage, and he is a real person—just like you are—with his own thoughts and feelings and plans and these may or may not align with yours. It's important to remember that your focus in this stage should be just on having fun and enjoying each other's company, because one of the worst things you can do right now is get ahead of yourself.

We already know this guy is attracted to you and doesn't detest your company because you've been out a few times. How you act in this stage can determine if you scare the shit out of him, if the two of you mesh well, and whether or not you're going to be compatible long term. Which leads us to a very important topic . . .

The Dangers of Emotional Masturbation

WTF is emotional masturbation (EM)? Well, we all know what physical masturbation is and both of you will (hopefully) have done that at some point in your lives. Bros are very likely to do this in the early stages of dating and you can bet by the time your first date is over a bro has already had sex with you in his head.

Women, however, tend to masturbate much more frequently but in a different way. Instead of fantasizing about having sex with him, *emotional* masturbation is stimulating your brain by fantasizing about everything from him impressing your mother to how his name will look on your wedding invitations to what private school your kids will attend . . . all before you even get to the second date. The one little trick for successful emotional masturbation is this: Don't fucking do it, ever.

When you let your mind wander off into a fantasyland where the two of you are happily married with two kids and a Cavalier King Charles in the yard, you're setting yourself up for disappointment and twisting what you guys actually have into something fictional.

You don't know that much about this guy yet. He could be totally insane,

> *"Don't put the penis on a pedestal."*
> —The Betches

weird, a douchebag, or just generally not boyfriend or husband material. But, when you set him up to be the perfect man you're creating an unrealistic and ridiculous image of what you want him to be, which he can't possibly live up to. You end up disappointing both him and yourself because it turns out he's not interested in working in finance while you vacation with the kids in the South of France.

He's a real person, and real people are complicated and have nuances and aren't always whom they immediately appear to be when you've only spent about eight hours total with them. So please stop envisioning your kids as legacies at Wharton.

Emotional masturbation is another reason to put off having sex with someone too soon. When you have sex with a bro, your body releases oxytocin, a "cuddle" hormone that makes you want to be closer to the person that was just inside you. This is stronger for women because in the age of cavemen it was biologically advantageous for women to form stronger bonds with their sexual partners so that men will stick around and raise the baby that their NuvaRings couldn't eliminate. Putting off having sex with a guy until you're comfortable around him and more sure of his feelings will help you curb your EM.

On top of all this, indulging the fantasy can blind you to this guy's obvious, or even not so obvious, flaws. You're so obsessed with him wifing you up that you brush off the fact that he says he's an atheist when you're from a religious family, that he continuously hints that he's just looking to fuck around right now, or that he's currently rewatching every episode of *Desperate Housewives* and absolutely loving it. Be realistic about this guy's shortcomings and don't make excuses. Don't be desperate enough for a boyfriend that you'll let anyone who checks off the boxes of tall, dark, and douchey think they're worth your time. Sure, give him a chance. But

as always, when he shows you his true colors, pay attention, and if he sucks, quit while you're ahead.

Also realize that there are many commitment-phobic men out there, especially in their twenties, who aren't looking for anything serious. They may be open to the idea, sure, but they're definitely not actively looking for it, and the odds of you being the one to make them realize the power of true love are pretty fucking slim. And even though you can practically hear the vows he will say to move your guests to tears at your getaway wedding in Capri, it's not going to change his decision that he's not ready for a serious relationship. Instead, your absurd fantasies will just make it that much more painful when and if he eventually pulls away.

Dear Betches,

I've recently met a super-hot pro with whom I've really hit it off. He's a total gentleman and has asked me out on a few dates, and things have been going great. Over the weekend, it was his friend's birthday so we all went out to the club together. After a hot night of drinking and dancing I finally let him take me home. Everything was going great until he took his pants off . . . this guy is small down there, and quite significantly, might I add. He's literally the smallest I've ever seen, and so the sex was bad. I don't know what to do, as I really like this guy and he's awesome in every other aspect.

This situation is fairly recent however, so it wouldn't be too late for me to back out since I haven't developed any major feelings yet. But honestly I do want to keep seeing him because he's a fantastic guy in every other respect. My question is: Is this something I can/should deal with, or will I just become more bitter about it over time, so it's best to end things now? I know you can't decide for me, I just wanted to get some advice/general knowledge from you as my besties haven't been much help in that department.

Sincerely,
Too Small to Please

Dear Too Small to Please,

Discovering that a guy who's otherwise great has a small penis is always a letdown. These guys also often have pretty good personalities because they need to compensate for something. Take comfort in the fact that even though your guy isn't physically cocky, he isn't personality-wise, either.

Unless you're Samantha Jones, I've never heard of someone harboring secret bitter resentment toward someone else for having a small penis. Like, a small engagement ring—definitely, but I can't remember the last time my bestie told me about a fight with her boyfriend where he was like, "Could you be nicer to my mom?" and she was like, "Can you grow a bigger dick?"

That being said, if the sex is bad and unexciting, the relationship is going to suck. There are plenty of ways for a guy to make up for the fact that he's not well-endowed. If he's not pleasing you with sex alone, make sure he goes down on you or finds a position where he can get in deeper. The small penis thing shouldn't be a dealbreaker unless he sucks at all other sexual shit, too. Most guys know how to make up for their sexual limitations. I'm sure he's not operating under the delusion that he's huge. If he doesn't make sure you're sexually satisfied, that's a different story, and in that case you should break up with him. Sex is an extremely important part of a relationship, and if it's not good now, it's going to really suck once you're two years in and things aren't fresh anymore. And hey, in the words of Larry David, it's possible that you just have a big vagina.

Sincerely,
The Betches

SPARK NOTES

The time between casual dating and defining the relationship can cause a shit-ton of anxiety. Does he like me or does he *like me* like me? Why hasn't he returned my texts in under ten minutes? *He's totally ghosting me!* On the other hand, it's easy to let your mind wander to places it hasn't yet been invited to wander. You can get caught up in a fantasy relationship that doesn't exist. This is harmful because it stops you from seeing who the real person in front of you is, receding hairline and all.

At this stage the most important thing to do is stay calm and NOT get ahead of yourself. Try and stay in fun, casual mode and the guys will come running. In general . . .

- Show a guy who you are without scaring the shit out of him. This means not overreacting to things, playing it cool, and *slowly* revealing personal information about yourself.

- You can and should keep seeing other guys at this stage of the game. He has every right to see other people until you guys clarify that you're exclusive.

- Don't stalk him or even follow him on social media. It's best to not know what he's doing

when you're not around if for no other reason
than it's none of your fucking business yet.

- Don't emotionally masturbate. He's just a regular guy: Don't make a life for the two of you
  as a couple when you don't even really know
  him yet.

5

Making It or Breaking It

The Dating Process

Now that you and your guy have both decided you're not just hooking up, this is the stage of your relationship when it gets tricky. Why? Because of all the uncertainty of the future of you as a couple and, of course, the increased pressure to buy new outfits (at this point, you've already worn all your good ones). As a betch, the latter won't be hard at all, but the former will be somewhat complicated. Now's the time to figure out if he—and this relationship—is what you actually want while also maintaining your mystery. Here, we'll let the Head Pro explain.

Chill the Fuck Out,
He Is Not Your Boyfriend Yet
by Head Pro

Everyone—male, female, vegetable, and mineral—bemoans "the Game." "I'm tired of the drama and playing these games!" you wail. "Why can't I just tell a guy I like him? Why can't a guy just come out and say he's not interested?" This is what people who are bad at the Game say. And yet, for all the pissing and moaning people do, wishing they could just wear their feelings as T-shirt designs, do you know anyone who actually does it? Do you know anyone who runs around happily fucking everyone they want, blissfully free from the shackles of conformity? And no, Lindsay Lohan doesn't count, mostly because she traded the shackles of conformity for actual shackles.

There are people who think they do, though, the "I'm over/too old/too good for playing games" types. You know these girls. You may even *be* one of these girls. If you show me someone who hasn't put some version of that in an online dating profile, I'll show you someone who's never used the Inter-

> *"When you really don't like a guy, they're all over you, and as soon as you act like you like them, they're no longer interested."*
> —Beyoncé

net, because they're like, eighty years old. These people, to put it bluntly, are full of shit.

Saying "I don't play games" is just another form of the Game, and not a particularly clever or truthful one at that. That's because just about everyone misunderstands what the Game is. For a lot of misled girls, the Game means being willfully obtuse, playing hard to get for the sake of playing hard to get. For the kinds of men who hang out on men's rights activist message boards, the Game is trickery, manipulation, and outright hacking a woman's brain into giving up all that sex she's being so stingy with. You may view these types as being very sad, despicable people. You are not wrong; they are wrong about the Game.

The Game is not lies. The Game is how we convey to the opposite sex the way we want to be viewed without being so overt as to say "I am a cool guy, please touch my boner." The Game is marketing. A sales pitch, much like nearly all facets of human life. An ad for a Chanel bag is 90 percent about appealing to the lifestyle you wish for yourself, and 10 percent about showing the actual bag—it's why they can charge you thousands of dollars for thirty dollars' worth of leather. When you apply for a job, you don't scrawl *AM GOOD WORKER, GIVE JOB YES?* in red crayon on notebook paper—you send in a resume that's pages of

> *"A rich man doesn't need to tell you he's rich."*
> —Neil Strauss, *The Game*

trumped-up bullshit (no, Karen, going to Canada to get shit-faced on your eighteenth birthday doesn't count as "international experience") intended to sell you to the employer as a total package.

You know that guy who comes off as shady, the guy with slick lines who never answers text messages in a timely manner and always "has plans." He's telling you exactly how he wants you to perceive him: He's an in-demand guy who can't be tamed and doing so will require a lot of sacrifice on your part. The girl who "doesn't play games" is simply telling guys she's a cool girl who's not like other girls, because she thinks that's what men want to hear. Can the message be deceptive? Sure. Sometimes Mr. Shady Bro is just a loser who's never known the sweet caress of a woman. Sometimes Ms. No Games plays a *shitload* of mind games once she has a guy interested. Sometimes diet pills are just capsules of sawdust and broken dreams. The difference is, the FCC doesn't field complaints for false romantic advertising. I know, I've tried.

We all play the Game because it's unavoidable—virtually everything we do is intended for consumption by others, and thus passes through our own internal PR departments. The Game is advertising. The Game is branding.

The Game is all of us. So let's play.

HOW TO DEAL WITH BEING GHOSTED

You've been hooking up with some guy for a little while and so far it's been pretty good. You guys meet up drunk at bars with your friends a few weekends in a row, he sleeps over several times, and texts you throughout the week to see how it's going . . . all signs seemingly point to a continuing relationship. The next week rolls around and suddenly he stops texting you. Just like that. No fade-out, no one-word responses, no lame excuses not to chill like, *I'm in desperate need of a haircut* or *My boy is hosting a pregame this week*. Sorry Betch, but you've been ghosted.

There's a big difference between being ghosted after one date and being ghosted when you've been on a handful of dates and ~~likely~~ perhaps have already emotionally masturbated yourself into a "relationship." The short story is that one hurts much more than the other. When a guy ghosts you after you've been seeing each other for a while, it hurts a lot fucking more because you take it more personally. "But I thought we had a connection!" you cry. Maybe you did, maybe you didn't. Much like the existence of God or the nutritional benefits of juice cleanses, you'll never know what's up for real so it's best not to overly concern yourself with the "truth."

So what do you do? For one, you definitely don't berate him with "??????????" texts. That'll definitely make you look like a fucking idiot. Not only will he not respond, but he'll show his friends his phone like, *Yo this chick won't leave me alone, good thing I dodged that crazy bitch*. What you have to do is mentally cope with the fact that it's over. You've got to let go, Jack, you've got to let go.

Here's how:

Step One: Accept it

As with any type of emotional wound, denial comes first, therefore acceptance is always the initial and most difficult obstacle to overcome. But you're a betch and if you were/are able to black out four nights a week yet still graduate college in eight semesters, there's nothing you can't handle. Remember, he's just a dude who has fucking issues of his own. Shit happens.

The last thing you should be doing is sitting around waiting for him to text you. Not only will that drive you insane, but also it'll stop you from actually moving on and make you super boring. Closure is for ugly people.

> *"Just because I tasted her cum or spit or could tell you her middle name or knew what record she liked, that doesn't mean anything, that's not a connection. Anyone can have that. Really knowing someone is something else. It's a completely different thing, and when it happens, you won't be able to miss it, you will be aware, and you won't hurt or be afraid."*
>
> —Adam, *Girls*

Step Two: Figure out why, but don't dwell

Once you've accepted that it's over and he's not going to text you, you're probably going to start replaying the entire "relationship" (that wasn't) over in your head until you want to vomit. Despite how many times you tell yourself not to, you will, so we'll just explain how to make it quick. Go over everything that happened, but don't be one-sided about it. It's very possible you did something wrong (or at least something he didn't like), and if you did, it's almost easier to move on because you can learn from your mistakes.

This is obviously much easier for those who are smart enough to self-reflect. For those who aren't, we don't know what to tell you. Call your mom.

Step Three: Move on

About fifty percent of the time it's not you, it's him. This guy clearly wasn't—and therefore isn't—worth your time. Even though the reason for the ghosting could have been your fault, it could also have had absolutely nothing to do with you. It also could have been a combo. Either way, don't be upset about some nobody. Go work out, go shopping, go out, and get drunk. Go do what you need to do to make yourself feel super hot because you are (unless you're like, not). Betches don't have time for people who waste their time, remember? Move on!

Here's a tip: Always have two to three guys on deck. This way when one pulls away, you don't feel as bad and you're still getting attention from one to two other guys. Just don't have sex with all of them. That's super slutty and will emotionally fuck you up more than if you saw like, an actual ghost.

YOU WERE NEVER REALLY DATING: GETTING OVER THE ALMOST BOYFRIEND

Now for the opposite of ghosting. What's worse than the guys who disappear? The Peter Pans of the world who string you along for months—sometimes years—giving *just enough* to make you hope they'll materialize into relationship material. Despite *Sex and the City*'s best efforts to convey otherwise, this NEVER happens. Once it becomes clear that this guy does not want anything serious, it's your job to recognize this and move on. Which leads us to the dreaded Almost Boyfriend.

These shady guys are the ultimate mind-fucks betches must deal with in the dating world. They are not just booty calls, because they say nice shit to you and treat you somewhat like a girlfriend, but will maintain a level of shadiness that keeps you wondering who they're texting when you're not around. Enough of this shit. We love mind games, but there is definitely a line that he is crossing with this kind of asshole act. Have some balls, girl, and say what you want. No one likes a coward.

Here are five signs you've gotten tangled up with an Almost Boyfriend:

1. He says he doesn't want a girlfriend, fucking duh.

Look, if this guy flat-out tells you in the beginning that he is not looking for a girlfriend, that is a pretty good indicator of how things are going to go down. This remains true, even if he's whispering sweet nothings (ew) and making tons of plans with you. If you think there's even a chance that you're going to catch the nastiest disease of the season—one-sided feelings—just bounce before it even gets to that point. We don't care how well you play the Game or how great your blow jobs are—if he hasn't decided to make you his girlfriend after three months *max*, he probably never will. When he says, "I don't want a girlfriend," he's really saying, "I don't want *you* to be my girlfriend." It's as simple as that.

2. He doesn't introduce you to his friends.

If he's always talking about his friends but you have yet to meet any of them, that is a red flag. Not a red flag like his friends are imaginary (that's possible, too) but this move is like *Yes, I have a life besides you, and no, you can't be a part of it.* He probably doesn't mean this consciously, unless you're hooking up with a super-villain narcissist, but subconsciously that's what he's saying. Get out now.

3. He doesn't care if you mention or go out with other guys.

If a guy wants to wife you up, he will not be chill with the thought of you flirting with other bros. Of course he wants you to have a life of your own outside your relationship, and he trusts you when you hang out with your guy friends, but if you mention that your trainer looked super hot today and he doesn't flinch at all, then he probably doesn't care that much about you. Even more obviously, if he's talking about dating or going out with other girls in front of you, he doesn't want to be with you seriously. Note, though, that the opposite of this doesn't necessarily mean that he wants you to be his girlfriend—it's possible for a guy to treat you like shit, but *also* be possessive.

4. He gets really evasive when you try to casually ask where things are going.

This should be an obvious one, but if you've tried the "LOL the other day my mom saw your pic and asked if you were my boyfriend and it got me thinking . . ." and he just aborted the fuck out of that mission, that doesn't mean he didn't understand what you were getting at and you need to have a sit-down talk. It means he quickly apprehended and dodged that bullet because he does not want to have that DTR convo, maybe because he does not want to DTR. If he's avoiding commitment talk more fervently than a *Say Yes to the Dress* marathon he is just not that into you. Sorry, no offense, but it's true.

5. He lets you go too easily.

If you've broken things off, and he was just like, *Let's be friends* and *Do what you've got to do* (ugh), it's a sign you should go running—in the opposite direction. If a bro likes you and sees somewhat of a future, even if it's a date to his cousin's wedding, he's not going to give you up without a fight. That is, he'll ask you to clarify what went wrong and try to rectify the situation, not accept it faster than you can write a term paper on Adderall.

If any of these signs look familiar, he's an Almost Boyfriend and it's time to cut this guy out of your life. The longer you let this guy linger, the harder it will be to get over him and move on to guys who actually want to be with you. It's obviously easier said than done, but so is anything worth doing (see also: planning a trip to Belize, perfecting your maid of honor speech, finding the right manicurist). You want a guy who is fully into you and who feels lucky to be with you. If he's wavering, it means he's not "fuck yes," so don't even waste your precious time on him.

Warning: Once this guy realizes you are moving on, he may up his game and try to get you back. The thing about guys who don't want to commit to you is that they're equally unable to commit to NOT being with you. Once he feels you pulling away, like clockwork, he shows more interest. If this is the case, his failure to commit is more about his own personal issues with commitment and intimacy and less to do with him not liking you, but that's not your problem. His issues are his own shit to work out and betches don't have time to deal with someone else's indecisiveness or relationship problems. Don't fall for that. Remember what Maya Angelou said.

Inspirational Scene from *Bridesmaids*

Ted: I'm just, you know, I just have a lot coming up at work.

Annie: Oh!

Ted: And...and...and I just, I don't wanna make promises I can't keep. You know what I mean?

Annie: Mmm.

Ted: I know you do.

Annie: Yeah. We're on the same page. I mean, I'm not looking for a relationship right now either. Let's just say that, I just...whatever you wanna...I can do, you know? I'd rather just...I like simple. I'm not like other girls like, "be my boyfriend!" Unless you were like, "yeah!" Then I'd be like, "maybe."

Ted: But that's not on.

Annie: I don't want that either.

Ted: I don't either.

HOW DO YOU ELIMINATE HIM FROM YOUR LIFE DESPITE THE FACT THAT YOU LIKE, REALLY DON'T WANT TO

All the fugly people of today's generation complain about how our dating culture is on the verge of extinction because of how many weird "in-between" labels have developed. In fact, *Vanity Fair* basically dubbed Tinder as the downfall of modern dating and an end to monogamy. It states that online and app dating have caused men to stop treating women like priorities and instead like swipe-a-fucks, who are replaceable and unimportant. In our opinion, this is only true if you let it be true. Men will treat you with the respect you demand. If you're fucking any guy that buys you a drink on a Tinder date, this may ring true for you. If you're selective about getting to know people and eliminate the assholes who are just there for ass, this need not apply to you.

There's talking, there's together, there's exclusive, there's dating. But what they're not saying is that these types of relationships are becoming prevalent because we're allowing them to be. So what people need to do is have some balls and speak up for what they want. Maintaining an air of mystery and not giving a shit are musts, but when it comes to acting like Almost Boyfriends are acceptable then you need to participate in a new kind of Ice Bucket Challenge (#tbt). The cause is called WAKE THE FUCK UP. Dump some ice-cold water on your head and stop being an idiot.

You shouldn't be tolerating in-between behavior. It's totally okay to have a bro you like to hook up with when you're bored and no one else is around—that's what we call a back-burner bro—as long as both you and he have a mutual understanding of what your relationship is and definitely isn't. But it's not okay to lie to yourself and say you're completely fine being just friends with benefits when you actually want more. Own your feelings. It's lame and pathetic to lie to all your friends and yourself. Once you recognize that you've emotionally masturbated this guy into someone whom he will never be and that he is simply not that into you, you only have one option: Cut the cord.

Say no when he suggests canceling your dinner date to watch a movie. Turn off the Taylor Swift and ignore his Snapchats and Instagram likes. Ignore his eleven p.m. texts suggesting that you "should chill this weekend" that never prompt any follow-up plan-making texts. Remind yourself every time you get a seemingly random check-in that you deserve to be someone's priority, and this bro obviously has not made you his.

This guy can tell you a hundred times over that you are witty, gorgeous, smart, kind, sexy, fun, and every other adjective for amazing, but you have to believe it and accept it yourself. If you truly believe you have these qualities, you won't fall victim to guys who use their words instead of actions to convey their feelings. Talk is literally the cheapest thing you can do. It costs no money and requires no effort. Words are bullshit. If you really want to see if a guy is into you, look at his actions. You want to be with someone who takes your life into consideration, who plans dates ahead of time, who goes out of his way to be present in your life. If they don't demonstrate that they think they are lucky to be with you, you will never be treated the way you deserve to be.

You need to acknowledge all the moving pieces in this puzzle of your pseudo relationship with him and learn from it for future relationships. Figure out what it is about this guy that makes him a bad match for you and the reasons behind why you're attracted to guys like him in the first place. Next time you'll be smarter about the guys you let yourself have feelings for. If you do it right, these realizations and growth will be big stepping-stones in your life, and you will use your experience with him in so many more ways than you can even imagine right now.

Finally, delete his fucking texts, e-mails, and notes. Believe us, the word "'sup" doesn't magically change into "I've loved you all along" after the fifth read. Don't tell all your friends that you're done with him. They don't give a shit. Just be done with him. Be confident, brave, and independent. Don't look back, Betch, you're on to better things.

> "Work hard to make something as beautiful and meaningful as you can and when you're done, pack it in and know it was all temporary."
> —Yoga Jones

What Would Karen Do?

Karen assumes a guy she's been on five dates with is her boyfriend and tells everyone they are together. She takes the lead on all aspects of moving their relationship forward, suggests he meet her parents before they're official, and generally tries to tangle his life up with hers in every way imaginable before they've even defined anything. When he inevitably gets scared off by this, she uses her forced friendships with his friends to stalk him and pretend that it's a coincidence that they are still at the same parties and events.

SO WTF *DO* I DO?

So WTF do you actually *do* while dating a guy who hasn't agreed to be your boyfriend? Good question. The most important thing: Continue to date other people. You're not exclusive yet? Date other people. Are you like, not sure if you're exclusive? Date other people. Did you DTR, but he pretended not to hear you and asked to see another picture of your cat? Date other people.

Shit Crazy Bitches Do: Assume Exclusivity

Never assume you are exclusive unless you two have explicitly spoken about it. If your friends ask you "OMG are you guys exclusive yet" and you're like, "well . . ." or say "yes" when you very well know you aren't, then you are what we call a Delusional Dater or DD. In other words, you've officially entered crazy town. There's *no assuming* when it comes to exclusivity. When you assume, you make an ass out of you and me. When a friend asks, "How are you and your boyfriend?" and he hasn't called you his girlfriend yet, tell that friend "Ohhh he's not my boyfriend yet" coyly and change the subject. If you're overconfident or lying to yourself and others about the subject, you will feel fucking dumb when you find out the bastard hasn't even saved your number in his phone yet.

Dating others benefits you in many ways. Namely: 1. You will be distracted from Bro One's lack of attention for you; 2. Because you will be distracted, you won't give him as much attention, making him believe you're not that into him; 3. If he somehow finds out that you are seeing someone else, he will become jealous and he will become even more into you than before.[3] When dating a guy you really like, nothing narrows your perspective more than not having back-up bros to think about.

Second to dating others is focusing your energy on something other than men. Don't stress about bros 24/7. Don't think if you don't have a boyfriend today you won't be engaged in two years. Don't shush people because it's noon and you need to concentrate on your new Hinge matches. Love happens the same way as the lottery and herpes: when you least expect it. So chill the fuck out, sign up for aerial yoga, join a gym and never go, or try SoulCycle three times then yell off the rooftops how riding a yellow bike to nowhere has changed your entire life.

But for fuck's sake, stop obsessing over that one guy who said hi to you that one time. It reeks of desperation and no perfume can cover up that stank.

---

[3] This is hard to maneuver without looking desperate and ruining everything. Just one forced Instagram will end it with Bro One. Please do not attempt if you are not a seasoned manipulator.

> ### Shit Crazy Bitches Do: Get Obsessed with Engagement
>
> Ever see a nicegirl post an article online titled "5 Reasons to Get Engaged Before You're 23" with the caption "Totes agree!" This is the DTS, or the girl who's Desperate to Settle and she makes us cringe. She has Pinterest boards filled with her future wedding decorations and seating arrangements. Shit, she probably prays at night for the perfect man. Don't be this girl. If you have to be a Pinterest girl at all, be the one with pictures filled with chic throw pillows or zero calorie wine. And if you're going to pray, pray for these things, too.

Third on this list of shit to do so you don't die alone is giving into the Game (but realizing that it's actually only a game). We went into a lot of detail about the rules of playing the Game in *Nice Is Just a Place in France,* but a lot has changed since 2013. Either society has changed in the last few years (example: with iPhone texting becoming more like a chat, it's now okay to double text within a thirty-second span of time) or we have gained a slightly more mature (key: slightly) perspective on life. Either way, the Game exists for a reason: to play it.

There's really no point to go into very specific advice with case by case scenarios because there is one overarching rule that applies to almost every single situation when playing the New Game. It's called: Hold the Fuck Back.

Did he text you that he thinks you looked cute today and you so badly want to tell him *OMG I saw you looking at me you looked so cute too do you wanna come over? I'll cook you dinner and we can call my mom and tell her we're getting so close!!!* No, bitch. Hold the fuck back. Text him back: *Well thanks. I mayyy have noticed you looking cute today, too.*

Did he follow you on Instagram and you so badly want to like all of his pictures and comment on every single one of them with the boy/girl kissy-face emojis or inside jokes? No, bitch. Hold the fuck back. This is the lowest form of flirting, equivalent to a Facebook friend request. Would you comment on his pics there and message him a *thanks for accepting*?? NO, you wouldn't, because you're sane.

Did he invite you to his frat party or a friend's pregame and you so badly want to come alone, buy the most expensive bottle of wine the liquor store has in stock, stand by his side all night, and bring a large bag containing all your sleepover essentials because you assume you're going to cuddle tonight? NO, BITCH. Hold the fuck back. Show up with two friends and talk to other people until he comes over. And bring vodka.

While resisting showing outward affection slash borderline obsession at the beginning of a relationship is important, it's equally important to resist inward tendencies, too. This is where Emotional Masturbation comes in, and this is also where it stops. An occasional fantasy about a hot guy staring at you in a subway or a casual daydream of a lower-middle-class-but-at-least-you'll-have-a-happy-life with your gorgeous Starbucks barista are okay in theory, imagining how cute a guy with whom you've been on three dates is going to look changing the diaper of your firstborn is totally crazy. The barista doesn't fucking care if you're crazy, he's still going to make you your trenta iced coffee. The guy you're dating, however, will dump you the moment he even senses you're becoming too obsessed. Keep the fantasies to a minimum and your reality in check before you emotionally masturbate yourself off the relationship deep end.

Shit Crazy Bitches Do: Send Unwarranted Heartfelt Messages

Shit like *thinking about you, can't wait to see you, wish you were here* are all normal to send to your boyfriend, but not to someone whom you want to be your boyfriend. Your boyfriend will respond, *Can't wait to see you, too, babe.* A man who is not yet your boyfriend will reply, *Lol same* or *Who's this?* or he'll simply say nothing. Holding back your emotions via text before commitment or his initiation is key to keeping the relationship and flirtation on course. It keeps you mysterious. It keeps him guessing. It keeps you in the Game.

The vice versa applies here as well. Imagine a bro drunkenly texts you *I miss you I can't stop thinking about you* after you've only gone out with him twice. You'd laugh, show all your friends, say *whooaaa stalker* to your bestie, and then show the texts to everyone you know for the entire week afterward. While your ego is glowing, you're totally going to move on from that weirdo because too much too soon is disastrous. So, next time you want to text him *miss you cutie,* imagine him showing your text to all his friends and them all laughing at you for days.

This is all not to say that you should be an emotionless robot when dating. Just the opposite, actually. Be funny, cute, flirty, sexy (not to be confused with sexty). Be yourself. Just don't be your craziest self. He has a lifetime to hang out with that girl once he's like, totally fallen in love with you. It's all just a matter of when to show him all your sides. He won't be able to get to know that funny cute flirty sexy betch if he sees the oversharing, too-eager girl first. Remember: If you show him all your cards before the Game ends, how will you ever win?

Do I Get My Besties Involved?

It's best not to get your friends too involved in your relationship too early. Sure, you may have the urge to set your friends up with his friends so the two of you have more reasons to hang out, but you are not an official couple yet and intertwining your worlds too soon could make it awkward if shit doesn't work out. Limit the friend intermingling to bringing your besties to his pregame and keep your worlds relatively separate until you've discussed that you guys plan on making this a long-term thing. Don't let your friends friend him or get otherwise involved in his world. It may scare him off; as with most other stuff in early dating, let him take the lead.

SO YOU'RE DATING A
PSYCHO . . . DEALBREAKERS
IN CASUAL DATING

When you're in the "casual dating" stage of seeing a guy, it's easy to ignore red flags in favor of your own fantasies. But overlooking things you know to be warning signs can result in you getting deeper into a situation with someone who may or may not be a commitment-phobic narcissistic psychopath, a.k.a., Mr. Big from *Sex and the City* or Scott Disick.

Many guys seem normal at first until you find out they're compulsive liars or misogynists, but the good thing about allowing the realization to break through in the early stages is that the stakes are still low enough to get out before he ruins your self-esteem and life. Here are some examples of the types of guys that could fuck up your mental space so much that you find yourself drunk-crying at a bar or worse, questioning your own sanity and hotness.

> "So, I assume you've come here to make arrangements. But unfortunately, I don't fuck losers."
>
> —Kathryn Merteuil, *Cruel Intentions*

The Liar

Some men lie. A lot. They lie about how tall they are, how they think you look in that dress, their feelings for you, going out with their friends when they're really on a date, fucking other people, etc. Some guys lie just to get out of an uncomfortable situation or to spare themselves the awkwardness of telling you how they really feel. There's a word for these men and, as much as we hate to use it, it's the only fitting word: Pussies. A man who cannot grow the balls to at least tell you to your face that he "didn't have sex with that girl" or "*accidentally* liked all his ex's profile pictures" is not a real man. He's a boy who is scared of facing his problems head-on and not someone you should continue to deal with. If he's lying to you in the beginning of your courtship, he will definitely lie—and lie bigger—once you two are committed. Relationships are built on trust, and you cannot trust this guy for shit. Time to run.

> "Clinton lied. A man might forget where he parks or where he lives, but he never forgets oral sex, no matter how bad it is."
>
> —Barbara Bush

The Emotionally Abusive Womanizer

This guy cannot help but try to have his cake and eat it, too. There are some men who simply feel hemmed in regularly fucking any fewer than three women at a time. When you try to call him out on this behavior or ask why he takes two days to return a text, he will try to turn the tables and call you "clingy" or "psycho." When you break up with him because he won't commit, he'll text you at two a.m. hoping you're drunk and tell you he misses you only to fall back into the same evasive pattern of assholedom the next day. His ego feeds off of any attention you give him so he'll try to milk that attention for all it's worth given the slightest opening. He is a narcissist and has deeply rooted issues involving his inability to care about the feelings of anyone besides himself. Best to block his number, he is bad news and extremely toxic.

The Talker

From the way this guy talks about you and your future, you'd think you were married by now. He is constantly complimenting you and saying extremely nice shit to you, but here's the catch: His actions don't reflect the talk. Despite texting you daily, he never asks you to hang out. On occasion he'll ask you to come over and watch a movie or catch up, but he never puts any real effort into your dates. He considers himself a "nice guy" because he speaks respectfully to you, but he never follows this up with any actions of importance. This guy is the worst kind of time-waster and it's up to you to dodge his manipulative words and cut the shit. Next!

> *"Actions defined a man; words were a fart in the wind."*
> —Mario Puzo

If you encounter any of these guys, it's time to run. If a guy has committed any of these crimes he's committed the ultimate sin: He made you waste two to six nights out on him. Drop him like the fly he is and make room in your life for quality men who put in the time and effort to show you how amazing they know you are.

Inspirational Fictional Betch: Belle

Gaston: It's not right for a woman to read. Soon she starts getting *ideas,* and *thinking* . . .

Belle was a hot nerd who loved reading and didn't give a fuck about guys. All she cared about was like, her library card and her dad. Lame, but whatever. For some reason, hot jock Gaston was really into her whole virgin vibe and was trying to wife her up. Belle wasn't an idiot, though, and knew that if she married Gaston he would treat her like shit. Eventually she decided to accept a date with the Beast who, although ugly-hot instead of hot-hot, was rich as fuck and had some pretty good game. If Belle can get over the whole "my boyfriend got me to date him by kidnapping my dad and holding him ransom and then locking me as a hostage in his house" thing, you can probably have a pretty nice life with an ugly-hot bro once you get to know him and he proves he's going to treat you right. Hell, he might even be so happy to be with someone out of his league that he buys you a whole library and some antique clocks and shit. Moral of the story: Don't discount nice, rich, fugly dudes. Also, you're much more likely to meet a guy while actively doing shit you care about than hanging out at taverns with hot assholes.

Dealbreakers from a Guy's Perspective by Head Pro

Hey girl, let's talk. This stage of the relationship, the part where you're "not like, technically a thing, but it's definitely going somewhere" is the dealbreaker-iest level in the video game of dating for guys. Hell, for some guys, the very state of having an almost girlfriend is itself a dealbreaker, but those guys are damaged souls and not worth fretting over. For everyone else, here are some traps to avoid if you want a shot at that sweet, sweet "girlfriend" label.

Texting/snapchatting all the fucking time: Girl, I spend like, two nights with you every week. Can a man live?

Getting weirdly, irrationally jealous: It's one thing if you see me out somewhere talking to another girl and casually ask who she was the next time we hang out. It's a whole other thing, when confronted with this situation, to physically put yourself between us, literally pee on me and shout "we're sleeping together" while maintaining eye contact with the other woman. THAT'S MY FUCKING BOSS, WHAT HAVE YOU DONE??

Trying to make him jealous to "tip the scales": I get it. Some guys refuse to get off the pot, but you're 100 percent sure that there's no shitting going on. In that instance, you might be tempted to flirt obviously with other guys in his field of vision in order to make him "see what he's missing." Don't. Sure, it *could* work, if the guy you're dealing with is a spineless weenie. But if you're dating a quality dude, all he's going to do is feel hurt, get pissed, and flip it back on you. In that case, all you'll have done is waste a substantial amount of time and an incalculable amount of emotional energy.

Pressuring him to meet your parents: Point-blank, if there's no *explicitly stated* exclusivity, nobody needs to meet your parents, your cousins, or your fucking high school history teacher. It's the same mentality as the above dealbreaker: *If I foist [milestone] upon him, he'll come around.* That's not how it works. Throwing an infant into a pool won't turn it into the next Michael Phelps.

Getting all stalkerish on social media: The girls explain this in greater detail elsewhere, but at no point do you and a guy need to get all that cozy on social media. That's especially true at this fragile stage, where you might feel tempted to insert yourself into his virtual life so other people know you exist. Do not do this. People will be like, *Haha Jake, who's this girl commenting on your mom's birthday Facebook post?* and you're not going to like his answer.

Inviting yourself everywhere: Sure, at this point you might be in a place where your dates/hangouts are implied, which is great. You meet for drinks every Wednesday and Friday, spend your Saturdays together, etc. However, don't get into the habit of inviting yourself along every time he mentions an activity on his calendar. He'll feel obligated to include you, and obligation is what you feel for your dentist, not for your almost girlfriend. Just because he's going to crush brews with his bros on Sunday, it doesn't mean he'll forget about you.

Getting hit by a bus: Sorry, we can't wife you up if you're dead.

Hi Head Pro!

I need some advice. I've hooked up with this guy a handful of times and am starting to develop some feelings for him. (Hence, me spending x amount of time writing this e-mail to ask for advice.) This guy is the type that is super attracted to bold and confident girls. I'm a big believer in the guy being the one to pursue the girl because, call me old-fashioned but, if he wants it bad enough he would, right?? So I've been playing hard to get like it's my job, but he doesn't really make that big of an effort with me. Normally I would classify that as a "he's just not that into you" situation but this Friday my friend was talking to him at a party and he asked about me and she asked him why he hadn't approached me at the party. He responded with, "Well she doesn't really respond to my texts/Snapchats so I don't really think she's interested in me." My friend responded that she doesn't necessarily think that's true, but that I just like to play hard to get and be pursued. He goes back, "Well I play hard to get, too."

Is it really possible that two people can game play this hard-core with each other, or was his response just a cop out and he's really not that into me?

Give it to me straight up!

Sincerely,
Serial Gamer

Dear Serial Gamer,

Jesus, where to start? First, it's intellectually dishonest to fuck a guy a few times and call yourself "old-fashioned." Second, you seem to have a very fundamental misunderstanding of what it means to "play hard to get." For instance, in no way does "playing hard to get" or "being old-fashioned" conflict with being bold or confident. It also doesn't particularly describe the situation you've found yourself in, where you hooked up with a guy and then decided there was something to be gained by ignoring all of his attempts to contact you.

"Playing hard to get," for the uninitiated (and we *are* initiated, aren't we, Serial Gamer?), describes the means by which you keep someone on the line. It's the push/pull, the give and take that occurs in a fledgling relationship (and even a mature one, if you know what's up). It's communicating pleasantly with someone, but not agreeing to go out on a date just yet. It's dating someone casually, but not being DTF right away. Basically, it's creating positive experiences and reinforcement for someone, but leaving them wanting a little more each time until they're sufficiently invested in you as a person. It behooves both men and women to do this.

Guys view intimacy as linear, also known as the "escalation ladder" in creepy PUA-type circles. First comes interest, then dating, then kissing, then sex, etc. Basic "sex as a baseball analogy" stuff. It theoretically works in reverse, too—if a girl will sleep with you, then she'll probably go on a date with you, too. By doing one but not the other, you've completely fucked with his whole paradigm. When his data set consists of a handful of hookups and a bunch of unanswered texts, his only conclusion is that he was wrong, you weren't really that into him and it was just a fling.

It's not an issue of you both playing the Game too hard as much as it is you trying too hard to play the Game incorrectly. If you like the guy, you kind of have to work with him a little if you want him to know you're open to being pursued. The Game isn't hard if you're playing it right.

Elusive kisses,
Head Pro

SPARK NOTES

The period of time after you've started dating but before you DTR can be nerve-wracking for both parties. Your relationship has no label, but you're both enjoying each other's company. That said, there have been no claims of exclusivity so you cannot and should not expect anything from this person. Thankfully, this also means you don't owe them shit. Here are some key points to remember when navigating the treacherous time before the guy you're dating puts up an Instagram official photo of the two of you:

- NEVER assume exclusivity or anything else about your relationship. The Game can be a powerful tool in not coming on too strong and to ensure that he's still chasing you.

- If you are ghosted or otherwise broken up with during this stage, move on promptly. Don't try to salvage anything. He did you a favor.

- Eliminate toxic Almost Boyfriends who won't commit. After a certain point, a guy will either want to be with you exclusively or not. As they say, shit or get off the pot.

- Don't bitch about the hookup culture being the reason for your failed relationship. People treat you as well as you demand to be treated.

6

Lock that Shit Down

Getting into a Relationship

Congrats, Betch, you've decided you like this person enough to spend a lot of time with him and be in an actual relationship. Hopefully, you're positive he likes you just as much or even more. This is no small feat as finding a guy worthy of your affection is about as easy as figuring out how to use Reddit.

We can't stress this enough: The biggest relationship faux pas is assuming you're exclusive.

You'll always feel and look like a fucking nut job when you realize it wasn't the case. So then how do you know if you should be hooking up with other bros or if you're not the only girl on his radar? So happy you asked because it's really not that hard.

Exclusive or Not Exclusive, That Is the Question (of This Chart)

He's wants to be exclusive	He (probably) doesn't want to be exclusive
He asks you out for another date in the same week.	He asks you out on a date to his couch at ten p.m.
He asks you how your day is going.	He asks you what you're wearing.
He wants to get breakfast with you in the morning.	He wants to get head in the morning.
He tells you you are really smart and beautiful (duh).	He tells you your thong is really hot.
He snapchats you pics of him making bored faces at work.	He snapchats you pics of his dick at work.

Why did we put the "probably" in parentheses above? WHAT DOES IT ALL MEAN!? Calm down, psycho. It means that if he does the things in the "Not" column, it may not necessarily mean he doesn't want to be exclusive; it could either mean he's clueless or a more overtly sexual person. Which is fine. However, if he doesn't *also* do the things in the left column then erase the "probably" because he's not looking to settle down with you anytime soon.

A note on if your guy happens to fall in the "Not" column, without the *probably*. Ask yourself, can you maintain a casual relationship while knowing this bro is dating other people? If yes, then continue hooking up with him. Realistically, if you ever wanted to be exclusive in the first place, the answer to that question in most cases is almost always fuck no. But since betches are so amazing at manipulation, sometimes without realizing we end up being the victims of our own mind-fuck. We tell ourselves that we're chill and can totally handle this. NBD.

But all of a sudden you find yourself interpreting each and every one of his texts like you're in the NSA. *He used only one Y in hey this time. OMG is he in the hospital or something!?* So like, yeah you have a problem. You're no longer the chill girl you thought you would be. You're the anti-chill. You're the tepid girl, the one who wants the guy who clearly showed you he doesn't want commitment, to commit. And you created this problem for yourself. You let yourself get too deep and now you're drowning in a fucking pool of tepid water where no one will save you except self-reflection, a new guy, or your therapist. Sorry, betches have a flare for drama. But it's true.

Don't cry. Your life isn't over. Think about all the free time you'd been spending analyzing eleven p.m. "hey wanna hang out" texts. *OMG he texted me! But it's kinda late. He was probably working. Ugh he's such a hard worker. How long do I wait to text? He's prob gonna open a bottle of wine, so it's def considered a date. OMG shit I have to shave!* You have all that time back now. You didn't lose a potential boyfriend because this dick was never going to be your boyfriend in the first place. And if you think you can change that by doing things that you think he likes, that's just desperate and you've just lost your chance at ever sitting with us.

Let's rewind a bit. After reading the chart you've come to the conclusion that he probably wants to be exclusive, but now your problem is that he's still not initiating the talk or introducing you as his girlfriend. What do you do? Sometimes this guy needs a little nudge in the right direction. *My Big Fat Greek Wedding* taught us two things: Women with big noses can find love, too, and it's easy to convince a man to do what you want if you make him think he came up with it himself.

How you should NOT initiate the exclusivity conversation:

- Use your whiny voice to ask him *Are you my boyyyyyyyfraaaand yaaaatttt??*
- Text him *Like, are we exclusive or what?*
- Drunkenly text him *Are we exclusive or what because I'm about to hook up with someone. You have 5 seconds to respond.*

Instead, if you truly feel confident that he also wants to be exclusive, you should bring up the subject by making him the slightest bit jealous. Let's say he's going away for the weekend or going out for a big night with his friends. You're having a lighthearted conversation with him about it and you casually mention *Soooo are you gonna hook up with like, all the girls this weekend?* The delivery is really important here; if you come off serious or like a psycho, this will backfire. If he gets your sense of humor he will hopefully answer you *Haha no and the same goes for you.* If he sort of laughs it off and doesn't say anything, then either he's awkward or you should reevaluate the chart.

However, if you are not confident in this approach, in his desire to date you, or in your own ability to be sarcastic then you should try a more traditional method: The Adult Conversation.

Ughhhhhh, adulthood. Here's what you do:

What: You're going to ask him about being exclusive.

Where: In person, at dinner or drinks.

When: When he's in a good mood.

How: You have to be super light and flirty about this. Do not come on too strong but be confident in yourself. Start with, "So I'm not trying to have any serious, drawn-out conversation about our relationship right now, I just want to ask you something." He will most definitely get nervous so don't pause for too long. If anything diffuse the tension by laughing and be like, "Haha calm down I'm not pregnant."

Then say, "We've been together for a while and I want to know where you stand on us, specifically about dating other people." And that's it. Let him go from there. Even if there's an awkward pause—and there might be—hold your ground. Do not feel the need to ramble incessantly about each and every one of your feelings. You were adult enough to bring up the convo, it's his turn to tell you his opinion on the matter. Just give him like, the same level of intense eye contact you'd give a girl wearing kitten heels, until he feels uncomfortable and understands. If he asks you what you think about it, be sincere and straightforward. Refrain from screaming I DO!

Above all: Remain breezy. Go with something like "I mean we get along really well, and I have a good time with you, so I just want to know what your thoughts are about it." If he's not a total asshole or deathly afraid of commitment then he will most likely give you an honest answer.

Why: Stop asking me fucking questions.

Before you go and say, "But why do you automatically assume that we are the ones who are desperate for exclusivity?" Because, loser, if he'd asked you or brought it up first, then you wouldn't be reading this shit for actual advice. If you have to ask, you will most likely NOT like the answer, but better to find out before delving too deeply into your own fantasy life.

In reality, you should strive to be the girl to whom bros ask the tough relationship questions. Don't forget, you're a betch, you have a reputation to uphold. You value your hotness and uniqueness. There's no other girl who has your specific combination of cute, funny, confident, and perfect pores. You want to be that aloof betch who has guys lined up and down blocks to date you. Are super-elite nightclubs cool because they let everyone in? Um no, they are super selective and charge guys a shit-ton to even get in. Consider yourself a club and be picky about the relationships you enter. That's the girl you want to be, and that's why you should read further.

DEFINING RELATIONSHIPS IN THE TWENTY-FIRST CENTURY

These days there are many, many ways to lock down a bro and define your relationship that are way more accurate than just saying you're "dating" or "in love" or some other gross bullshit like that. So the next time you're about to fall asleep and some bro whispers "What are we?" into your ear, break it down for him with one of these more modern definitions.

Flirting Not Fucking: FNF

This is the dude who you text regularly, you like each other's shit on Insta and if you do end up in the same room there is a 90 percent chance you'll sit on his lap at some point in the evening, but you know you're never going to fuck him. Some people call this the "friendzone" but FNF is more than that because you're not really friends. You just hit him up at random times (usually when another bro is pissing you off), flirt, and then let him go back to whatever it is he does when you're not gracing him with your presence. Occasionally when you're really bored you'll make out with him.

How it ends: Considering most dudes don't realize when they're your FNF, there's a high chance he'll try to actually hook up/define your relationship eventually. This will be sad and awkward for both of you. You'll never speak again.

Pretending You're Friends: PYF

This is the most common relationship in a betch's life. This is the bro who without fail will find his way into your bed and vag at some point between Friday and Sunday (maybe Monday, if it's like, a long weekend). You don't think about him too much, and you're pretty sure you like him but then one day your friend will ask you where he went to school and you'll realize you don't even know if he went to school, or where he's from, or if he has a family or a dog or a house or anything apart from a functional dick and a job that leaves him free on the weekends. A.K.A.: The Fuck Buddy.

How it ends: It never ends.

Makes You Psycho: MYP

All it takes is one decent dick with a bank account to turn a formerly bad betch into a psycho. One minute you're living the life, ignoring texts on the reg, and generally winning and the next you're making a bonfire out of some bro's undershirts and sending him late-night Snaps of you crying. You're updating your status with song lyrics and hanging around the shitty bars he frequents just so he can see you "being chill." The two of you fuck occasionally, and it's always really intense and then he leaves early in the morning (but you meet up at CVS a day later to go halfsies on the morning-after pill). Every betch has her very own MYP to make her feel so shitty that she has to start a cleanse just to get back to normal. It's like how there's evil in the world so that humans can know goodness. It just has to be so. You commonly identify him as an Almost Boyfriend, while to him you are "that girl who's good in bed but kind of psycho."

How it ends: You spend a month listening to like, a lot of Adele, get your shit together, and get over it. What doesn't kill you makes you betchier.

Technically Dating But You're Both Terrible at It: TBDY . . . oh fuck it

This a bro whom you somehow agreed to date exclusively and then almost immediately realized that exclusivity was a terrible idea for both of you. He's distant and busy and you DGAF and are still actively texting your back-burner bro. You always end up at the same place, but aside from these semiregular sleepovers you're basically just hooking up but with the benefit of being able to tell your grandma you have a boyfriend.

How it ends: One of you dumps the other, neither gives a shit.

WHY SOCIAL MEDIA IS THE FUCKING
WORST FOR RELATIONSHIPS

Trusting someone is hard enough as it is. It's like you're just expected to believe someone is good and not a shady piece of shit, even though you barely know them and most humans are at least partially shady. Fine, we'll go along with it; innocent until proven guilty. But proving someone guilty is a lot easier to do now that his trail of indecent behavior is available for your casual viewing pleasure.

Gone are the days when the only way you could catch your boyfriend cheating was physically walking in on them. Now we have to deal with new Facebook friends, friends of his posting pictures from "innocent" weekends in Nantucket, personal Snapchats, direct messages, the list goes on. And we're supposed to just ignore them? Fuck waterboarding, if you really wanted to torture a terrorist you should dangle his wife's sent and received Snapchat lists in front of his face and watch him confess in thirty seconds.

Like, one day you are happily single and love to go out. And the next you're happily in a relationship and love to refresh your boyfriend's Instagram following list. Could life be more unfair? Trusting him would come so much easier if his every move weren't available with just a click.

You might be asking, "How can you say you're happy if you're constantly looking for a reason to break up?" That's a really good point, bitch. But we have a better point. If you're not an actual psycho jealous girlfriend and just simply a curious one, it's natural to wonder what your boyfriend is up to.

You're not looking for a reason to break up, you're just giving into your urges to stalk your new best friend, the one whom you have sex with and who buys you dinner. The fact that social media is so huge just proves that people love to know what other people are doing, so wouldn't you want to know what the person whom you spend the most time with is doing when you're not around? Fucking duh.

On the other hand, there is a line between stalking and snooping and that line is called "his cellphone." Once you find yourself glancing at his texts, catching a Snapchat or two, or clicking the home button fake-thinking it's yours, you have crossed the line. And once you've crossed the line it only gets worse. Read: Actually going through his phone, signing on to his Facebook account, friending his exes, etc. These are all really bad relationship behaviors, and all are signs that you are the psycho jealous girlfriend who probably has serious insecurity issues and you must be stopped immediately.

In reality, snooping gets you nowhere. Unless you have reasonable evidence, as in you seriously suspect something shady is up based on something you saw (not based on previous ill-advised snooping), when it's almost sort of okay . . . but still definitely not. Most of the time you'll either find nothing or find something that may seem suspicious and will drive you off the deep end when really it was also just nothing.

We understand where you're coming from. You just want to make sure that your boyfriend, the person who is supposed to respect you the most, isn't making a fool of you. But unfortunately, you can't without disrespecting his trust. It's fucking annoying but true.

You're going to have to talk to him and be honest about how his behavior on social media makes you feel. When we say "talk" we don't mean accuse or verbally beat the shit out of him. We mean saying something like "I just want to make sure we're on the same page in terms of trust and where we are in the relationship. Like, would it make you happy if I took borderline inappropriate pics on Facebook with random guys? I bet not. YOU FUCKING ASSHOLE."

Just remember, he had a life before you, he had female Snapchat friends before you, and those female Snapchat friends will continue to send him Snaps. Until those Snaps are of her tits, you shouldn't pay them any attention. Instead, focus on more important things like sending him sexually suggestive selfies of yourself. (Calm down, we don't mean actual sexts. Just show a little cleave here and there. A kissy face can work if you don't look like a full-on platypus.) Keeping your sense of perspective will go a much longer way than accusing him of fucking all of his coworkers.

Instagram Official

Instagram official is the new Facebook official. It's weird how society changes so quickly, we know. As a betch, it's important to stay ahead of the social media game, because if you don't you're just going to be that super-weird girl in your bestie group circle who is like "what's Periscope?" and "wait,

I can make myself look skinnier through an app!?" Eyes will roll harder than a nicegirl on molly.

Why is Instagram official the new Facebook official? Because Facebook is passé. People care more about what you post on Instagram because each time you post you are saying something about yourself. On Facebook, people absent-mindedly upload albums of super-boring pics that all look the same, whereas on Insta, everyone knows you chose that picture because you think you look good, meticulously crafted that punny caption, and artistically filtered the shit out of it. #imsoclever.

So, posting a couples pic means just that, you're a couple. Unless everyone knows that you two are just friends then maybe they won't judge. But even so, you can't trust your followers to think sanely. Even with a pic of your guy friend Greg, friends and followers will be suspicious of a secret hookup or even worse, a secret but desperate crush in the air.

> *"Facebook relationship statuses are for losers."*
> —Anon

Shit Crazy Bitches Do: Post First

If you are extremely confident in your new relationship (as in your guy told you you should post the photo in a nonjoking way) that is the only time it is okay to post the couples pic first. If you have already DTR'ed and you are officially a girlfriend then you can also post it. But if you are in neither of the above situations, just don't. Either let him post first or wait it out until you don't need to think twice. You're a new couple, there's plenty of time to let the world know you guys like to go pumpkin picking together and are like, *OMG so eff-ing cute.*

Don't worry, you'll know when someone is in a relationship on Instagram, even if the picture is seemingly innocent, because a betch's friends will be so excited at the first couples pic that you can bet on them commenting with no less than three heart emojis (or saying shit like "OMG love this couple" if they're a particularly annoying type of human). Either way, you won't miss it.

YOU HAVE A BOYFRIEND: NOW WHAT?

Yay, you have a boyfriend. For the girls who are always fantasizing of that amazing moment when a bro becomes your boyfriend, sorry but it's rarely that exciting. When it's meant to be (not in the lame sense like destiny or anything, but meaning it just played out without any drama), there's not going to be some grand gesture or like, something out of a Katherine Heigl movie. The way it works is that you two continue going on dates, he does really nice things for you that show you he's really into you, and then it just keeps going like that. He's not going to show up to your apartment window in a trench coat playing Beyoncé on an old radio above his head. A) Where do you even get a fucking radio? B) You wouldn't even hear him; you live in a high-rise. C) He'd probably get arrested before you even noticed.

The point is that when it's right, it's easy. Of course there will be some bumps to get over and kinks to straighten out, after all, you two are just getting to know each other while you're having sex. There are bound to be some minor fights that stem from letting your guard down, opening up, learning to trust, and other bullshit like that. However, if it's hard at first—you can't seem to trust him or he can't trust you, he won't make any effort planning dates, or you don't want to meet his friends—these are all signals that you two should either talk about and resolve it or end the relationship before you get in too deep.

The more time you devote to thinking about him, speaking to him, seeing him, sending him the perfect selfies, etc., the deeper and deeper you get. This is a fact that freaks a lot of people out. *How do I know if he's right for me? What if he's not the guy I'm going to marry and I've wasted all this time in a relationship with him and I'll blink and be thirty years old, sad and single.* Shit, typing that even stressed us out. To answer these questions, here's what you do: Shut the fuck up.

Betches Throughout History: Eve

Eve was the first woman in the whole world, and even though she had very little competition she was obsessed with self-improvement. When the serpent told her that she would never die and could actually get hotter just by eating an apple, she totally bought it and was then kicked out of the hottest day spa, Eden, and sent to live in the real world with Adam for the rest of her life. I mean, that was way harsh, Tai. The lesson we can learn from Eve is that you have to love yourself fully or you can be deceived by slimy men who try to change you into something you're not. If you can't be happy with yourself then you can't be happy with your boyfriend, Adam, and you will have pain during childbirth and lots of other annoying stuff to deal with. Moral of the story, accept yourself and your flaws as they are because life is all about perspective. Also, there're a lot of carbs in fruit.

Am I Wasting Time on This Guy?

Unless your boyfriend is literally the worst, as in treating you like shit and making you feel bad about yourself, then you are not wasting your time. Actually not even. As long as you realize he sucks very quickly and dump him even faster, then you didn't waste anything. Instead you learned that you need to be more wary of the guys you decide to take on the role of your BF and not just let any douchebag bro in your heart and your La Perla thong.

You learn something about yourself with every relationship. So really, it's sort of like, a narcissistic thing, so we can definitely get on board. Like, every boyfriend is just making you a betchier you. For example, your first boyfriend didn't like to drink and was too shy. So you learned that those things didn't cut it for you, and picked someone for your next boyfriend who was a little more outgoing and liked to get blackout once in a while. Yay, more fun for you. Boyfriend #2 was great until you came to realize he really hated his mom (like, weird hated) so you moved on, realizing that you want someone more family oriented. Yay, you avoided a potential lifetime of fighting over how to raise your kids, but boo, no more talking shit about Susan. So for Boyfriend #3, you find a guy who is a genuinely good person and also likes to go out and is close with his family. You have yourself a keeper, but without those previous relationships, you may have never appreciated how lucky you got with the third.

But who knows, maybe you marry this guy and he starts gambling like, everything you own and runs over your dog or something. Shit generally goes down the drain. Sorry religious people, but divorce is no big deal. Being on your own should never be something you fear so your perspective during your relationship should ALWAYS be *Whatevs, what will be will be, and if it doesn't work out I'll be totes fine. But for now I'm having the time of my life so I won't waste one more minute worrying that he's not The (nonexistent) One.*

Sex: Definitely Have It

There's a reason why every Real Housewife of Wherever the Fuck will say the key to any marriage is sex and also blow jobs: It's true. At the start of a relationship, you may not be comfortable enough to suggest things you want or the way you want them. That's natural. However, the more you get to know and love each other, that wall should crumble and you should feel more free to say whatever you like without the fear of him judging you. If he's your boyfriend, he thinks you're hot and he wants you to be happy, so he'll probably want to do what gets you off. If you still feel uncomfortable bringing something up after several months of a relationship, you should probably talk about it with a professional because, bitch, you have a problem.

Simply put, the whole point of a relationship is that you trust and respect each other. If you don't trust that he won't laugh at your suggestions or you think he doesn't respect you enough to listen to what you need, then you're not in a healthy relationship. Dump him.

Boyfriends want sex. Good boyfriends want you to enjoy sex. Unless you're like, trying to stick anal beads up his ass, which will probably be a comfort thing not a respect thing, he's going to be okay with it. Then again, a lot of guys are up for whatever, so even if you're like, into pegging, it probably won't hurt to ask. But we imagine it won't NOT hurt, either.

Let's back it up a bit (pun always intended). What if he wants to do things with you that you're not comfortable doing? To be honest, you never know what you may be into, so you should probably try most things once. Like we said before, if there's trust and respect, he won't do anything that makes you truly upset or unsafe. Have a glass of wine and a safe word. Try something new, but keep in mind, there's always a difference between a little dirty talk and him calling you a fucking slut. A lot of girls are into the former, some girls are into both, but few girls are into the latter. If your boyfriend happens to like something that crosses a line for you, speak the fuck up.

Sex should be enjoyable and—more important—mutual because do you know what another word for one-sided sex is called? It starts with an R and rhymes with crêpe.

So that we don't end this section on sex on a weird assault-y note, let's just say this: The more sex and better communication you have, the happier you will be. It also like, makes you emotionally closer to your boyfriend as well as relieves stress and releases endorphins. And endorphins make you happy. Happy people just don't shoot their husbands. They just don't.

Is He a Good BF?

As we said before, you're only kind of wasting your time if this guy isn't treating you like a fucking queen (you remember, because you're gaining self-knowledge, the only kind of knowledge that matters). But just in case you're on the fence, here's a guide to help you figure out if he's one of the good ones.

Good	Questionable
He calls you every day.	He texts you every other day.
He introduces you as his girlfriend.	He doesn't introduce you at all.
He plans dates and dinners.	He invites you to pregames.
He smokes weed sometimes and asks you to smoke with him.	He smokes before he brushes his teeth every morning.
He wants you to meet his friends.	He drunk-calls you and says mean things when he's out with his friends.
He puts up a pic of you two on his Instagram.	He comments on Nicki Minaj's Instagram, "dat ass doe."
He asks, "How was your day?"	He asks, "Can you get me some coke?"

Don't think that betches can't be one of the bad ones, too. Just because you have a left-column guy doesn't mean you have the right to be a right-column girl. While we are never too shy to admit we're fucking amazing and any guy would be lucky to have us, we have to feel and act lucky to have them, too. If he treats you like Bey, you should treat him like Jay. Never take what you have for granted because it can disappear faster than you can take down a vodka soda. Once in a while you should plan a surprise date, insist on paying for his entire dinner, give him a level-10 blow job. If your guy is capable of appreciation, he surely won't ignore you trying. Once he sees your effort maybe he'll go down on you more than usual, send you flowers randomly, or agree to watch *The Bachelor* with you. Swoon.

I Love You . . . I Think

After several months of dating this bro you start to get like, super-serious feelings for him. Like the kind that brainwash you into thinking it's okay to go on a date with him tonight, even though this is the third *Real Housewives of New York City* episode you've missed this month. But with love, everyone is different. The only consistent rule is when to say it: Never before the guy does.

That may be antithetical to our advice to be confident in yourself, but whatever. If you're 100 percent positive he loves you and you've convinced yourself that he's just a little shy and that you should say it first, then go for it. But we're writing this book for you, not him, so we have to inform you that your little confession of love turns the tables a bit favoring his side. Because if he doesn't say it back, your entire world will indubitably fucking collapse. You'll hate yourself for putting your emotions out there for him to destroy with his dick and his silence, and it will haunt you for the rest of your life, as in you will never tell anyone how you feel about them again. No big deal, right? But, if you're the confident betch you claim to be, then just do your best to be extremely certain that you will not be upset if the conversation doesn't go your way. Otherwise, it's just not worth it.

Think of it this way: Even if he does say it back, you'll always wonder in the back of your mind if he meant it and if you made it too easy for him. So it's sort of a lose-lose. We suggest waiting it out, and it will happen when you're both ready.

But what, you ask, if he says it when he's drunk? Haha that sucks. This definitely does not count. Think of the last person to whose face you said "I love you." (Family doesn't count.) Did you mean it? Prob not. Were you drunk, in a bathroom, bonding with girls whom you just met and made plans to go on Spring Break with? Definitely yes. Need we say more? If he gets wasted and is like "OMGGGG I just fucking love you," assume he was blackout and pretend it never happened. Don't bring it up. If he remembers, let him feel stupid and watch him awkwardly squirm.

Saying "I love you" is not about *when,* because it could happen in one month or six. It's about *why.* If you feel like you have all this love in your heart (barf) that you can't contain (double barf) and just want to tell this guy how you feel, then that's when you should say it. But, friendly reminder, it will fucking suck if you pour your heart out and all you get is an *awww thanks I love having sex with you!* in return. If you wait for him to do it, think of saying it back as a romantic gesture. Like, wow you're such a great girlfriend that you waited until you were really sure to tell him how you felt instead of jumping the gun. And for the record, "really sure" generally means when he has the balls to say it first.

What Would Karen Do?

Our darling delusional Karen would most definitely say it first and way too soon with like, emojis or written on a cake or something horrendous.

MEETING THE FRIENDS AND FAMILY: OH FUCK

The time has come for you to burst your relationship bubble. Now it's not just about the two of you anymore, but also about the other people in his life besides you. Ew.

For betches, meeting people is no big deal. We do it all the time. You know you're extremely charismatic, can put yourself together, and have a really attractive smile and nod. But that's not to say we like doing it. Being forced to meet people you don't know is like having to go work out super early in the morning; it's a fucking drag and you'd rather be sleeping, but there are benefits, such as not having to wait for an elliptical.

The Friends

The most ideal way this can go down is at a pregame. When it's not too loud, there's enough alcohol flowing that you'll look interested in topics you hate but not enough to get blackout and say something stupid as fuck. Also, there are enough people there that you won't have to linger too long during one conversation. (Getting out of a too-long conversation is about as comfortable as that quick postmanicure massage, you know, the one where they like, beat the shit out of you with their fists? *"Okay we done!"* But we digress.)

Laugh at the friends' jokes, playfully make fun of your boyfriend (in front of his face, of course) so that they see you're "a cool girl" and then maybe suggest a shot of Fireball or, ugh, whiskey. This is the only way to your guy's friends' ~~livers~~ hearts.

There's only one simple trick to your boyfriend making a success of meeting your friends: Have him buy them lots of drinks. They'll think he's sooooo dreamy.

IT'S NOT ME, IT'S YOUR FAMILY

The Parents

Meeting a boyfriend's parents is one of the more unnatural yet eventually necessary things a betch will ever go through. Obviously, the biggest annoyance is that you actually want these people to like you, which also requires pretending to give a fuck about things like making your summer productive or where your college major is taking you. Just pretend to eat whatever disgusting food they serve you, and seem reasonably down to earth and nice by answering all of their questions without saying "fuck" or letting on how long you've been having sex with their son. *"So how do you know our Steven?" . . . "He ignored me when we first met."*

The Problem of Siblings

Your boyfriend's brothers are like, whatever, it's almost the same as meeting his friends, but sisters are an inconvenient truth. A bro's sister is the only idea he has of what living with a girl would be like. If she sucks, position that shade so the lighting makes you look even better. If she's awesome and you're besties, congrats, you're in the real 1 percent.

Ultimately making a good impression is vital, because a bro's family members are just about the only people a betch can't tell him to get rid of. More important, though, every betch meeting a bro's parents should be constantly contemplating the big questions: *Are these people going to ruin every holiday for the rest of my life? What kind of family vacations in New Jersey!?*

So yeah totally, we want to put our best foot forward. But it's normal for meeting a bro's fam to feel like relationship judgment day, because you're getting a glimpse of your potential future. Is his dad hot? Is he like, kind of fat? Is the stepdad clearly a shady-asshole bro who flirts with the waitress? Is this bro rude to his family? Is he a flaccid mama's boy? Does he expect her to do everything for him? These are important questions. Nothing is worse than a dickhead who can't treat his family with respect. Dads of bros are a huge indicator of what you'd wake up to in approximately twenty years. And no betch wants to be second in command to her guy's mom, nor does she want to become her. Plus, if he's still got her packing him Snack Packs, he's probably lame in the sack, and you can't say we didn't warn you.

They say a good man is hard to find. Harder still is a good man with a cool mom. Mothers who believe that no one is good enough for their son are the Delusional Daters of parenting and will be a total drag. Betches are looking for a mom they can at least see eye to eye with, and ideally, a down middle-aged betch who turns water into wine-nights. Bonus points if you like his mom more than you actually like him. Hey, it'll happen to our future sons.

Remember that meeting your boyfriend's parents is basically a formality interview. Betches already have the job if they want it, but we look one hundred times better and make our lives ten thousand times easier by putting forth a little effort and going through with the interview anyway. And if it doesn't work out? Then, well, being the girl his family asks about forever is a hard job, but somebody has to do it.

Introducing Him to Your Parents

This all depends on what kind of family you have. If your parents are completely insane, like either still stuck in another century or mentally unstable, then you should wait until you have solidified your relationship to introduce him. You want to make sure that your mom saying "You remind me of a guy I dated in college" then winking does not cause him to break up with you. You want his reaction to be like, well that was fucking weird, but then laugh about it with you.

But if you have a somewhat normal family (no one's family is actually that normal, but, you know, comparatively) then invite everyone to a dinner to meet and go from there. Explain (calmly) to your mom that if she tells one embarrassing story about you she has no say in her grandchildren's naming, and if that doesn't work, tell her you're going to unfriend her on Facebook. It should do the trick.

It's up to you how much you want to help the boyfriend out. You can either give your guy some hints beforehand, like "My dad loves to talk about tennis" or "My mom will judge you if you don't order a second drink," or you can just push him off the metaphorical diving board and see what happens. On second thought, the latter sounds like so much more fun.

KEEPING YOUR GUY INTERESTED

The best way to keep a man interested is to have your own fucking life. Nothing kills a relationship buzz more than you two constantly in each other's faces, with you wearing two-day-old unwashed pajamas and your hair in a bun. You need to keep an air of mystery about what you're doing all day and who you're with. The betchiest way to act is to simply display that you're the shit and that even though you now have a boyfriend that's not a reason to abandon all the other amazing stuff going on in your life. Maintain your friendships, spend time with your family, don't give up hobbies you've spent years cultivating (a.k.a. spin class and binge-drinking).

But what happens if you're feeling your guy pull away? Does he not have the same urge to see you that he had when you first started dating? Is he overlooking important relationship conduct like texting when he gets home at the end of the night and paying for literally everything? How do you remind this guy that you are extremely valuable and that he could lose you at any time?

Your boyfriend needs to realize that if he doesn't constantly prove himself, there are dozens of guys on the back burner itching to take his place. And you are going to gently push that realization toward him. It's one of the most important tricks to master in a relationship. He should never think you are in the bag, in fact the opposite is preferable. He should have a fear of losing you to a worthy adversary at any moment. What's the best way to remind your guy that he's insanely lucky to have you and reel him in once he starts to get lazy? The following tried-and-true tactics toe the very fine line between subtle betchy manipulation and being a cruel bitch. It's an art, deal with it.

Ethical	Wrong
Not answering your phone when you're out with your friends.	Telling him you're going to fuck someone else when you're out with your friends because he hasn't proposed.
Having a bunch of guy friends who you text regularly.	Texting said guy friends after ten p.m. or saying anything explicitly sexual.
Being too busy to go to his grandma's birthday.	Being too busy to go to his grandma's funeral.
Doing drugs with your friends when he's not around.	Doing other bros with your friends when he's not around.

So the key here is to remain loyal and upbeat to your boyfriend while constantly reminding him that you have a very active life and he is lucky to be a part of it. There is no greater relationship killer than you focusing all your energy on someone and losing your independent side. I mean, if we wanted to date someone who was awesome, constantly around, and did whatever the fuck we said, wouldn't we all just be content with a dog and a fuck buddy?

What Would Karen Do?

She will choose her boyfriend over her friends every time. Her friends might ask her to come out with them this weekend but instead of saying yes right away, she checks if her boyfriend wants to hang out. If he does, well then, bye friends, hello being miserably alone when you inevitably break up.

SHITTY THINGS YOU SHOULD *NOT* DO IN RELATIONSHIPS

Of course the opportunity to actually date a betch is a blessing for any bro who is worthy enough (read: hot enough) to actually earn it. Betches are generally great girlfriends because they're not needy and they're not going to let themselves get fat just because they're not single anymore. That said, you know if you're making his life difficult. Here are the most common shitty things we tend to do in relationships that you should avoid. Or not. Up to you.

1. Do Not Have a Back-Burner Bro Who's Too Intense

Betches don't cheat. Cheating is not betchy. We do, however, let sad lonely dudes who clearly have crushes on us text us every day and make flirty little comments and make them live in the perpetual gray area of the not-really-friend zone.

The not-really-friend zone is for the guy whom you like to keep around to threaten and generally piss off your current boyfriend, while making sure that you have the added security of a dude who will comfort (read: fuck) you if things go sour with your current guy. You tell your boyfriend and all of your friends that he's "like a brother" to you and that you guys would "never" hook up, but everybody knows that is a lie because: A) guy friends don't exist and B) you are so fucking obvious.

When It's Okay: It's fine to have guy friends as long as you maintain certain rules, like not telling them intimate things about your boyfriend or letting them text you at inappropriate times (after ten p.m.) or things that are in any way romantic or sexual.

2. Do Not Set Traps

Setting a trap is a common way for a betch to blow off a little steam by getting in a quick midday fight with her boyfriend. They usually begin with a text about something random like, *Do you think I drink too much wine?* The key here isn't really the question, it's the fact that no matter what he answers she is going to be pissed, and she knew that when she sent the text in the first place. So if he says *nah u good* she's going to say *uh okay well actually alcoholism runs in my family. I know I've told you that. I guess that's how much you care.* But if he says *yah maybe slow down a little?* She's going to say, *oh okay but you and your dumbass friends can drink as much Jäger as*

you want and I'm not supposed to judge you? Have fun getting
fat, you fucks.

And voilà, now you and your boyfriend are in a fight and
you can force him to come over to "talk" until you both get
exhausted and have sex and fall asleep. This is known in the
betch world as, "A Typical Tuesday Night." Whether for
amusement or just to assert your female power, it's not actually a great idea.

Why it sucks: Because setting traps is for when you're trying to catch and kill something, not for your poor, dumb boyfriend. What else do people catch in traps? Mice. And what
do we know about mice? They're disgusting and too fucking
stupid to recognize a trap when they see one. They're going
to fall into it every time and then you have to call some
dude from your building to come over and smash it with
his shoe and then throw its body away. It's disgusting. Do
you really want to have to smash your boyfriend with a shoe
and throw his body away? If that's what you're into, there's
a really great way to smash the bodies of as many bros as
you want and then throw them away without even having to
initiate a text fight or anything. It's called being single. You
should try it.

3. Do Not Talk Shit to Your Friends

Everybody has had at least one bestie who is in a long-term
relationship yet has literally never once said something positive about her boyfriend. Any time you meet up with her

she's always talking about how annoying his friends are, or how stupid he is, or how small his dick is, yet when you see them together they are happy and, based on the frequency with which you accompany her to Planned Parenthood, the sex is fine. As far as you can tell, there would be legitimately no difference between how this girl talks about her boyfriend now, when they're together, and how she'd talk about him when they're broken up. This behavior is extra annoying, considering that there is probably a girl out there who would date him and like, actually like it.

Why it's shitty: It is your God-given right to talk shit about your boyfriend to your besties. Women have been doing this for centuries, or else we would have all gone insane before Jesus even got here. However, it only annoys the shit out of everyone to hear a girl constantly complain about a guy with whom she clearly has a fine relationship. And yes, there's a difference between asking your friend's advice and being an asshole. There is more important shit going on in this world for betches to talk about—like summer plans and abandoned acting careers—than bad-mouthing their boyfriends. Once again, if you want to fuck bros and then talk shit about them, there is an easy way to do that, and it is also called being single.

HOW TO FIGHT WITHOUT SETTING ALL HIS CLOTHES ON FIRE

Fighting with a guy is a staple of any relationship, especially a betchy one. This is where communication is most important and, if you consistently do it wrong, you will definitely fuck up your relationship and all you'll have to show for your trouble is a string of screenshots of his texts that you've sent to your friends in a blind rage as you get them all to communally affirm that he is, in fact, being an asshole.

Inevitably your guy will do things that annoy you. If he doesn't, you're either a doormat or you need to raise your standards. Guys do stupid shit all the time, it's their nature. Eventually you're bound to disagree over just how obnoxious that comment he made to your friend about her being "kind of slutty" was. Likewise, his irritation that you won't pay for a maid but will drop $700 on a pair of shoes is bound to bring up at least one mildly irritating conversation about your spending habits. Fights happen and inevitably lead to extraordinary make-up sex if handled correctly. Here's how to fight like a champion and come out winning *without* making your boyfriend cry under the covers.

Don't: Call Him Names

Telling your guy he's a fucking asshole every day is not really going to make him want to stop being an asshole. In fact, it might make him prove you right by acting like more of an asshole since you've already stated this as his major personality trait. Just like in that fight you had that lasted for four hours of texting about when he insisted he just said you were *"acting like* a bitch" not that you *"are* a bitch," you similarly want to steer clear of name-calling as it doesn't help anything. Never call your boyfriend a loser or assign unflattering signifiers on him. It's aggressive and, honestly, kind of too mean. The key is to make him *feel* like an asshole without actually assigning him that label. Which leads us to . . .

Do: State How What He's Doing "Makes You Feel"

Not to sound like fucking Dr. Phil, but telling a guy that when he doesn't answer your texts for four hours "makes you feel upset" as opposed to "is fucking rude" will make him a lot more sympathetic to your cause (even though it is really fucking rude). By saying how something makes you feel, it shows that you're not blaming him, reminds him that despite appearances you are in fact human, and teaches him the consequences of his actions. He can't argue with your feelings because they're your feelings (ew) and therefore not debatable. This makes the whole cause and effect thing easier to deal with, and is much more likely to make him feel like an insensitive prick—and therefore alter his rude behavior—without you actually having to come right out and say it.

Don't: Use Low Blows

Don't bring up shit that has nothing to do with the fight. There's nothing guys find more irritating than when you won't let something go. Two years ago he forgot your anniversary? Dick move, but that's no reason to bring it up when your current fight is about him getting a speeding ticket while driving your car. No one likes to rehash old mistakes they've made, and bringing them up will only make you seem petty, bitter, and unable to let go. Again, don't turn an argument about fidelity into an accusation about him being lazy or a chance to vent about how fucking annoying his friends are. Stick to the argument at hand, there's plenty of time to hash that other shit out in couple's therapy.

Do: Choose Your Battles

He insists on ordering in Italian food despite the fact that you told him fifteen times you're not eating carbs this week, goddamn it. Sure, it's easy to get irritable with the ones we love, but no one wants to be with a naggy bitch who turns everything into a fight. You have to learn how to chill out about some things because no sane man is willing to walk around on eggshells for their entire life waiting for you to explode. Save your meltdowns for important shit, like when your engagement ring is too small.

Don't: Get Physical

No. Matter. What. Never hit a guy. Your boyfriend would literally be dead if he ever laid a hand on you, and the same
respect should go to him. Most girls have had those drunken
moments when her boyfriend is being such a stupid fucking
idiot that you're convinced he needs to be betch slapped, but
even drunk, it's never okay. What are you, a Real Housewife
of New Jersey? Have some class. Control yourself and never
let yourself get to the point where you're manhandling him
anywhere other than in bed. Worst case scenario: Pull an
Elin Nordegren and just beat the crap out of his car.

Don't: Put Up With Gaslighting

Gaslighting is a term that comes from some old-ass movie
that means when a bro (or anyone, really—betches can gas-
light other betches) tries to deflect his or her own shittiness
by making you feel insecure and stupid, usually by telling
everyone you're crazy. A bro might do this when you've
straight-up caught him texting another girl and he calls
you "insane" because he thinks that will divert the attention away from him being a huge piece of shit. This is the
ultimate shady-bro behavior, but unlike other shady things
bros do, it's not attractive. Don't be fooled. Gaslighting is
bullshit and is used by people who want to take away your
self-worth to make you feel small, so next time somebody
tries it, tell them to fuck off. If a bro tries this tactic, he
doesn't respect you or any other women and you should se-

riously reconsider your relationship with him. Speaking of which . . .

Do: Know When an Issue Is a Dealbreaker

There are certain fights that are just too big to get over, and while it's entirely subjective, there are certain issues that should never be tolerated. This should go without saying, but if a guy consistently interacts with you in a way that's physically or verbally abusive you need to cut that shit out ASAP because, as we all know, not being in a relationship is better than being in a shitty one. Outside of abuse, though, there are a lot smaller dealbreakers that may seem like blips on the radar at the time, but are actually a really big deal. Here are some of them.

Red Flags vs. Dealbreakers in Early Relationship Stages

Red Flag	Dealbreaker
He openly farts in front of you after less than two months of dating.	He takes a shit with the door open after less than two months of dating.
He's constantly blacking out when you guys go out together.	He's blacking out and shouting at you when you guys go out together.
He calls his mom every single day.	He tells his mom about your sex life.
He admits to cheating on an ex-girlfriend.	He says cheating isn't a huge deal.

DEALING WITH HIS ANNOYING
AF TENDENCIES

So the honeymoon stage is over; it happens to all relationships eventually. Your guy's "chill" habit of leaving his shit all over your apartment floor becomes irritating as soon as you realize you might have to clean up after him for the rest of your life. His garage band, which once seemed like an artistic fun hobby, transforms into the big symbol of his lack of ambition to become the successful entrepreneur you always dreamed of marrying. The honeymoon is officially over, and you now can see what you've really purchased instead of what looked shiny and fancy in the store window, otherwise known as lust.

It's at this point in the Game that things get comfortable and, for many, with comfort comes boredom. The thrill of the chase is over, and what you're left with is the person you chose—flabby ass, hovering mother, and all. For some couples this stage comes later than others, but this is the point where you really have to ask yourself, is this a person I can see myself with for the next few years or—even more terrifying—for the rest of my life? Will this guy make a good husband, father, partner? Does he even know what a Naruto Roll is!?

You look at your boyfriend's flaws and wonder, *Am I settling? Or am I merely accepting the fact that no one (besides me) is perfect?* Is it okay to settle down with a guy who doesn't have a 401K? What about a guy not as hot as I am? Not as smart as I am? Someone who thinks a date at The

Cheesecake Factory is acceptable? Every betch has her individual standards, but where is the line between accepting someone's flaws and settling because you don't want to be alone?

The answer isn't simple, but it comes down to this: If, after years of being together, you're still excited to see your guy when he gets home, he treats you with respect, and you feel like you still have the same goals and values, and if he's a person whom you can trust and feel safe with, then you're probably not settling.

To be with someone for reals, you need to accept him just the way he is. If you want a puppy as a pet, don't buy a hamster. If you think you're going to change him, you're fucking delusional. If your guy's idea of affection is saving you the last pizza slice and you want someone who's going to bring you two dozen roses every week, it's time to move on. It doesn't mean he isn't a decent guy, it just means he's not for you. Everyone's version of settling is different, but if you're staying with a guy because you think his habits will change and he'll suddenly wake up one day the man you want him to be, you're setting yourself up for disaster and a lifetime of being mis.

But, if you feel in your cold, cold heart that you two have a good time but you can do better, let this bro go. You need to feel like you are lucky to be with someone, and he needs to feel lucky to be with you. If not, cut the cord. Let him find some other girl who actually thinks "That's What She Said" jokes are funny or who appreciates a guy who can party until six a.m. without calling.

Dealbreakers in Relationships
by Head Pro

Congratulations! Against all odds, you've connived your way into a 100 percent organic, locally grown, free-range artisanal relationship. Here are a few (but important!) things to keep in mind to avoid destroying the budding relationship with which you have been entrusted.

Cheating: Yeah, sorry, this is going to be a theme for the remainder of the book. You can't have your cake and fuck it, too.

Revealing any weird/calamitous skeletons in your closet: Okay, yes—the people whom you count among your loved ones are supposed to be the ones who accept you for who you are and support you through anything. That is true, yes, but in the context of a new, committed relationship, it would probably be best if he knew you were under investigation for tax fraud *before* he became your boyfriend. Planning a vacation to the Dominican Republic is romantic; having to change your destination to Haiti because you're wanted in the DR for murder is decidedly less so. The point is, if it's something life-altering, better to have revealed it earlier rather than later.

Getting up his ass about things that never bothered you before: Now, no one's saying that you're not within your rights to get pissed off if, at thirty-two, he's still coming home shitfaced every night like a twenty-two-year-old. But if all of a sudden once you become exclusive, you just can't fucking stand his friends, or the way he laughs, or his standing appointment with baseball every Saturday afternoon, that's going to come out of left field and he's probably going to be pretty hurt. You had every opportunity to air your grievances before now.

Picking fights for no reason: See "Setting Traps" above. We know exactly what the fuck you're doing when you do this.

Trying to make yourself a little too "at home" at his place: In fairness, this depends on where you are in your PMP, C++, Six Sigma Green Belt–certified relationship. But all too often, women assume "no, I'm not seeing other people" also means "feel free to make my place into your second home."

Any guy who doesn't let you keep some toiletries, makeup, and a drawer of clothes at his place is your boyfriend in name only, but there's a bright line between "couple" and "cohabiting." For men, their home or apartment is their sanctuary until the two of you decide otherwise. Do yourself a favor and stop image-searching for "throw pillows" for now.

Messing with his money: It's perfectly reasonable for you to not want to hitch your wagon to a horse who spends all his horse money like it's going out of horse style. A formal relationship is an important stepping-stone to more serious things, after all, so it's not a sign of good things to come if he's sinking all his horse dollars into carrot futures. But at this point in time, you're still two separate individuals, and what he does with his money is his business (and vice versa). If he can't pay the rent on the stable, by all means get out of the relationship, but don't give him shit for the occasional splurge. Like, have you seen your credit card statement lately?

CRYING: HOW TO DO IT WITHOUT BECOMING A NICEGIRL

We always say, "Tears are like lies." The more you use them, the less they're worth. Use your tears sparingly and only break them out when something is really, really distressing to you. Don't be that annoying girl who cries to her boyfriend because she saw him talking to some bitch at the bar when he was actually just asking a bartender where the bathroom was. Your tears are going to mean nothing if you deploy them all the time and they will indicate more how annoying you are and less you feeling genuinely hurt. Why is it so upsetting to see dads crying? Because it rarely happens, so we know someone or something must be really fucked up. Whenever you have a breakdown, aim for Dad Tears: seldom and restrained when necessary.

As a general rule, don't use your tears to make a guy pity you. He's going to think you're pathetic and this will only make him less attracted to you. You want your boyfriend to think of you as a confident, self-assured betch, not a weeping doormat. When you do use your tears, save them for a moment when something is not-overlookable to you so they make him ashamed of his behavior, not ashamed of you. For those of you who can only learn by example, here's one:

> "Pour yourself a drink, put on some lipstick, and pull yourself together."
> —Elizabeth Taylor

It's not okay to cry when: The waiter brings you yolks when you specifically asked for egg whites and your boyfriend refused to yell at him on your behalf.

It's okay to cry when: You're frustrated at the end of a fight after your boyfriend has royally fucked up and refused to apologize for it.

Generally, the more calm and cool you are during your fights the more power you will command and the stronger your argument will be when you verbally school him in why he is totally 100 percent wrong. Betches don't get sad, we get even.

> *"Don't get mad. Get everything."*
> —The First Wives Club

CHEATING: IS IT EVER EXCUSABLE?

The simple answer is: No. The more complicated answer is: Still no. Dealing with a cheater is pretty simple. If he can't be bothered not to stick his dick into some other girl, then he can be replaced. You're the prize, remember? Cheating is the ultimate betrayal and despite attempts at excuse or justification, there's never any excuse or justification. It doesn't matter if he told you immediately after. It doesn't matter if it was just one time. It doesn't matter if it was after you were exclusive but before he was officially your boyfriend. When it comes to cheating, don't be a fucking idiot.

If a person agrees to be in a monogamous relationship with someone else, then the very least those people can do is uphold the one major stipulation of a monogamous relationship. If you value yourself highly, then don't put up with people who do hurtful things to you, and cheating on someone is the most clear-cut, absolute violation of that agreement. How could you ever trust someone who would do something that is guaranteed to cause you an immense amount of pain?

But Betches, you might proclaim, *everyone makes mistakes! Don't we all deserve a second chance?!* No, Carmela Soprano, we don't. The kind of guy who would cheat, and especially the kind of guy who would cheat on YOU, doesn't respect you enough to not inflict conscious levels of pain on you and therefore he has G2G. Maybe he'll learn his lesson after you break up with him and maybe he won't, but either way it won't be your problem. The higher the regard you hold yourself in, the less disrespect you put up with from a shitty boyfriend. So no, you're not going to meet him on the Brooklyn Bridge and decide to forgive and forget like some delusional *Sex and the City* character. You're going to put on "Should've Said No," dump his ass, and send the clear message that there are some girls too great to give out second chances like they're Fairway coupons.

Occasionally you'll run into a bro who will give you a rant about how "unrealistic" monogamy is. If you're casually seeing or fucking someone with this opinion, it's time to run. Then again, at least this guy is being up front about his decision to not want to be exclusive with you. But, at heart, every guy who claims that there's "a biological imperative to spread his seed," really means that he doesn't think that you are worthy enough to be exclusive. As someone who knows she's the prize, you're obviously going to move on from this situation immediately for someone who is dying to lock you down, not negotiate terms and conditions to spout bullshit "evolutionary theory" about why men "aren't built for commitment."

Worse is the guy who tries to use this excuse after he has cheated on you. If you believe that people aren't meant to be monogamous, that's fine. Hell, maybe they're not. But if that's your belief, then just do what the above guy did, and be up front. Don't pretend you're into monogamy and then make a bullshit excuse about it afterward. That's called being a liar, and not even owning up to your shitty, weak actions, a.k.a. the worst kind of cheater.

Now that we've discussed what your tolerance for his cheating ways should be, let's move on to you, you shady betch. Many people wonder how far they can go with flirting before it becomes inappropriate. Can you accept a drink from a bro in a bar if you're in a relationship? Is it okay to even entertain a text conversation with a guy? Should you tell your back-burner bro to stop talking to you as soon as a guy locks you down? There's a fine line between avoiding being that boring loser who immediately starts every conversation with "I have a boyfriend" when she goes out and being a shady hoe who leads a bunch of guys on for attention. We've developed a handy chart to see which category you fall into.

Let a Girl Live	Shady Hoe-ville
Dancing in a group with girls and guys.	Grinding with anyone with a penis.
Texting a male friend for his section notes.	Texting a male friend that your boyfriend is being really annoying.
Accepting a drink from a guy at a bar.	Accepting a kiss from a guy at a bar.
Not telling a guy you have a boyfriend while you're casually flirting at a bar.	Not telling a guy you have a boyfriend after he asks for your number.

At the end of the day, the best way to decide if a behavior is acceptable is to ask yourself two questions before participating in any questionable activity:

1. If my boyfriend were here now and saw me doing this, how would he feel?

2. If I saw my boyfriend engaging in this behavior with someone else, would I be okay with it?

Unless your guy is a possessive freak, you can get away with being a chill friend and if he is a possessive freak, prepare yourself for a lifetime of having to explain that you're sorry that the Starbucks barista keeps asking for your number but you can't help it that you're like, really pretty.

THIS ISN'T WORKING OUT. HOW DO I GET HIM TO GTFO?

Now that we've established the dos and don'ts of communication in a relationship, it's time to evaluate if this is still a person you want in your life. Deciding to end a relationship that's not working is one of the toughest things a betch must deal with, like WAY harder than picking an outfit for brunch. Pretty much every relationship you have in life will end eventually—unless you or said person

> *"So it's gonna be forever or it's gonna go down in flames."*
> —Taylor Swift

die first, and even then, the relationship's over, right?—so the art of the breakup is definitely a useful skill to master early. The ability to do it gracefully and with tact will really show what a stand-up betch you are.

By breaking up with someone with whom you don't see a future when you realize you don't want them anymore, you're doing both of you a favor. Why would that guy want to be with someone who doesn't actually want to be with him? Set him free to find someone who actually likes him.

Also, breaking up with someone who you know isn't right for you shows that you respect yourself enough to not waste your own time trying to make something that you know is shitty work just because you're lonely or because your cousin Natalie's wedding is coming up and you don't want to deal with your grandma's rant about the drawbacks of dying alone. Some idiots will tell you that there is no right way to break up with someone, but that's bullshit. There's a right way to do everything: Our way. Here's how to break up, based on what stage of your relationship you're in when you decide you've gotta be free.

You've been on one to four dates and are not into him: You wait until the guy texts you and asks you to do something again. Then you respond with some variation of the following via text message: *Hey I had a nice time hanging out with you but I just don't feel a romantic connection.* If he has any dignity, he will respond thanking you for your honesty and wishing you well. If he's a little bitch, he won't respond, and if he's truly psychotic, he will write something mean back.

You've been dating two to four months but are not exclusive: You can either call him on the phone or meet up in person for coffee (don't expect him to pay). Tell him you've had a great time hanging out but you're not ready for something serious. Everyone who's not a fucking idiot knows this is code for the fact that you're just not that into them and very few will delve deeper. Say you hope you see him around and that he has a great summer/birthday/dental cleaning/whatever random bullshit he's told you is coming up in the near future. You then exit fairly quickly.

He is your boyfriend and you are exclusive: The breakup must be done in person, and you can share with him the actual reason that the relationship isn't working out. Don't use phrases like "I don't think I can do this," "It's not me it's you," or "I'm sorry. I can't. Don't hate me" without an explanation because if you've dated him long enough to be in a relationship he deserves a real reason, not some clichéd catchphrase you heard in a movie. Giving someone an honest answer for your rejection is the nicest thing you can do for them because it helps them find closure and then they won't feel betrayed or blindsided.

He's your husband: That's what divorce paper process servers are for, am I right?

I JUST GOT DUMPED. WTF DO I DO NOW!?

There comes a time in most betches' lives when they are on the receiving end of a breakup. I mean, even Taylor Swift has been dumped and she's six feet tall, blond, and weighs the same as she did at birth. Shit happens and getting your heart broken can make you into a stronger person and more resilient to challenges that come your way. Getting through the pain of a breakup can actually help you next time Saks is out of your size in the booties you're dying to have for fall. It's extremely painful to be rejected and you may be surprised at the horrible things that go through your mind as your brain scans revenge fantasies about him losing a limb, or worse, becoming obese (or whatever voodoo magic Adrienne Bailon did to usher in the current state of Rob Kardashian).

Depending on how long you've been dating a guy, the recovery period will definitely vary. During this trying time it's easy to become the most desperate, pathetic version of yourself but don't go there. Time and a hot rebound bro heal all wounds, and it's important to remind yourself that this guy was not right for you. If he were, he would never have let you go. Fucking duh.

> *"What doesn't kill you makes you stronger."*
> —Nietzsche and Kelly Clarkson, respectively

Here are some handy post-break-up etiquette rules to get you past the initial heartbreak:

DO	DON'T
Unfollow him on social media. No sane woman needs to see her ex's every move.	Stalk him or message him on social media. You will look psycho and desperate.
Cut off all contact. No texts, DMs, drive-bys, surprise visits to his bedroom window, etc.	Tell him that you are cutting off all contact. He will understand what's happened when you don't fucking contact him anymore.
Remind yourself of his worst qualities whenever you start to think about him. Think of his shadiness, his selfishness, the fact that he wasn't that attentive in bed, etc. If you can't think of anything on the spot, a simple "he ain't shit" should do the trick.	Stare at pictures of the two of you from when you were happy and smell the sweater that he left in your apartment.
Be pleasant if you run into his family or friends.	Try to keep in contact with his family. They're collateral damage of the breakup.
Say hello quickly if you see him at a party or bar. Then move on to talking to someone else immediately.	Hook up with him. Ever. Even if you're at a mutual friend's wedding and his hair looks sexy pushed back.

BREAKING UP OVER SOCIAL MEDIA

The social media breakup is a hurdle unfamiliar to previous generations of betches, and it can sting worse than an unanswered 12:45 a.m. text. When things end, either because you never really became official or because you ended your five-year relationship, social media can be a torture device unlike any other. Seeing pictures of your ex with others can make you go insane, and even seeing his newly accepted friend requests can send you into a stalking-rampage downward spiral. Most girls know the desperate agony of being up until three a.m. on the Insta of some girl their ex has newly friended in order to gain pivotal information, like the fact that she won her high school track competition in 2008. *Wow, he really traded up,* you think, downing your fifth glass of Cabernet. It's really not a good look.

When you break up, it's pivotal to do everything in your power to see as little of your ex's public information as possible. Nothing can ruin a perfectly normal day like seeing a Snapchat of him canoodling on the beach with a girl or being checked in by a stranger at that bagel shop that used to be your Sunday morning spot. Self-control has never been more important than in this phase of the relationship because without it you will drive yourself to a mental breakdown, or worse, turn into a Karen.

> *"Love is a fire. But whether it is going to warm your heart or burn down your house, you can never tell."*
> —Joan Crawford

Avoiding all his social media as much as humanly possible is ideal. If you look, the best case is that you find nothing and know the same things you knew before. Worst case, you see pictures of his new hot girlfriend and fight the urge to have a breakdown à la 2007 Britney. You're not Kylie Jenner, you can't pull off a wig.

Here are some good tips for social media breakups on the most popular apps of today. "So what," you cry, "are the rules for each site? They're all so different!" Calm down, Betch, we got it:

App	What to Do
Facebook	Stay friends with him but unfollow. This way you don't seem bitter, but you won't get any updates about him on your newsfeed. If you want to avoid poking your eyes out with your selfie stick, DO NOT go onto his page until you are fully over it. You can also unfollow his friends and anyone else remotely connected to him for extra security against seeing shit you definitely don't want to see.

App	What to Do
Twitter	Stay off Twitter immediately following your breakup. No one wants to read your sad quotes about "better to have loved and lost . . . " anyway, weirdo.
Instagram	Although unfollowing on Instagram is not a power move, sometimes it is necessary if getting reminders of him really causes you pain. If he's over you, he probably won't notice one less follower anyway, and if he's not it'll drive him crazy that you can't see his updates.
Snapchat	Unfollow. He won't notice unless he's obsessed with social media and in that case, you should be glad to be rid of him anyway. The last thing you need to see is a Snap Story of him in South Beach at his friend's bachelor party.
LinkedIn	Why the fuck are you looking at LinkedIn, nerd?

WHAT IF HE TRIES TO GET BACK TOGETHER WITH ME? SHOULD I LET HIM?

On-again/off-again relationships are rarely functional, and we highly discourage them. Would you Rent the same dress from the Runway over and over again? No. If a guy breaks up with you, he has majorly fucked up. But in our personal experience, all guys come back, in one form or another. And why wouldn't they? You are perfect, and he thought he could discard you. He needs to be punished for that. It can be tempting to get back together with a person who made you feel feelings and then bounced, but it is generally a really shitty idea. That said, it's your life, and sometimes recycling to keep your number low is a thing. Your decision to take him back or not should be based on your answers to the following two questions.

1. What is his reason for why things are different this time? Ask him. If his answer is that he's lonely or that he thinks you guys had fun together, then *fuck that*. If he feels like he's in a place where he's more mature and he tells you that he deeply regrets his decision and majorly fucked up and is willing to be ten times better to you, you might be able to entertain the proposition. But you should only even think of letting yourself go there if the answer to question 2 is yes.

2. Do you feel like he is really special and could be the one that got away? Never get back together with a guy who dumped you just because you are bored. Get a hobby if you're bored. You never want to be someone's back-burner bitch, it's not a good look. Unless you feel like this guy is seriously one of a kind and you'll never ever meet anyone half as great as him, then you should tell him to fuck off. Word to the wise, though: Be honest with yourself. It's tempting to just do what seems easiest in the moment when you're not thinking about your long-term future. Take like, three seconds to really think it over.

Bottom line: Don't get back together with your fucking summer-lifeguard fling. You're better than that.

One last note: If, after careful contemplation, you *do* decide that this guy is EXTREMELY LUCKY and deserves another shot, don't tell him that immediately. The best move here is to say you'll think about it, and then let him start from the beginning and date you from square one all over again. God forbid this guy should think that he can have you and dump you whenever he wants, like some sort of New York Sports Club gym membership.

> *"I wrote you 365 letters. I wrote you every day for a year."* (TBH, there's no mail on Sundays, but you get the idea.)
> —Inspirational rebound bro move from *The Notebook*

Betch, you are Soho House. Once a guy has unsubscribed, you can bet it's going to be fucking hard to get back in. You need to make him grovel, or he won't realize how big of a fuckup he's made. No one should ever think they could have you whenever they want, so he better have a plan for how much better things are going to be this time. You're a VIP, you're Beyoncé, remember? Would she take that shit? We think not.

Side note: It's best not to put out *at all* during this time.

Endearing Habits vs. Annoying Habits by Head Pro

Habits are like assholes; everyone has a few of them. You can argue about what, exactly, makes men and women "different" until the human race has reduced Earth to a lifeless crag hurtling purposelessly through space, but at the end of the day we can all generally agree that each sex has unique quirks. Some of those differences can actually constitute what makes us alluring to the opposite sex, while others are annoying enough to make us wonder why they even exist. Whether inherently feminine or just the byproduct of a sexist-ass society, the following are examples of quirks that men find endearing (or at least tolerable) while dating, versus behaviors that make us want to jump into a volcano.

Endearing	Annoying as Fuck
Asking us which pair of shoes, earrings, etc. you should wear even though you don't actually care what we say.	Making us late because you can't actually decide which pair of shoes, earrings, etc. to wear.
Suggesting we have a "guys' night," even if it's really so that you can have a "girls' night."	Saying it's cool if we have a "guys' night" and then texting us every five fucking minutes asking what we're up to.
Taking a little longer to look extra hot for a special night out.	Monopolizing the bathroom for four hours so we're forced to shave in the kitchen sink.
Appealing to our manly sensibilities by letting us drive/lead/navigate.	Making us drive and then bitching about our driving the whole time.
Venting/confiding in us when you've had a rough day.	Getting mad at us when we try to actually solve the problem.
Wearing something attractive at the expense of comfort.	Ruining our good time by complaining the entire night about how your feet hurt.

Endearing	Annoying as Fuck
Being cute/snuggling/ smooching during a movie.	Talking so much during a movie that you make us pause it to tell you what just happened.
Mixing things up by suggesting that we go out of town for the weekend.	Packing fifty pounds of shit in five suitcases for a two-night trip.
Catching us up on all the gossip going on in your office or friend group.	Talking so much shit about your "friends" that we wonder why you hang out with them at all.
Asking us what we think about your new outfit.	Asking us if your new outfit makes you look fat.

Dear Betches,

My relationship problems belong in a Shakespeare play, and I need your advice. I have been dating the same guy for the past five years and I am so in love with him. He's my best friend, has a nice car, and buys me expensive presents. The problem is, he cheated on me . . . multiple times. This past time it was with a girl he basically had a sober relationship with—dinner dates, multiple sleepovers, etc.

My friends tell me I need to ditch him and move on, but I can't bring myself to do it. He's a few years younger than me, so I think he just cheated because he is young and dumb. Here is the other problem— this is a secret relationship. My family doesn't even know we are dating. My family is very strict and has high expectations for me, and my boyfriend just doesn't meet their qualifications (he is a different race than what my parents want for me, never went to college, works in a fast-food restaurant, etc.). My parents met him years ago when we were just friends, and they hated him so much I can't even say his name in my house.

We have to sneak around like Romeo and Juliet. I lie about where I am going, where I am sleeping, the miles on my car, etc. Essentially, just a whole bunch of lies, and now I don't know where to go from here. I just graduated college and am ready to start my adult life. I want to tell my parents about my boyfriend and live a normal, public life with him. My question is: Should I confess about my secret boyfriend? And if so, how and what should I tell them? I can't ask my friends for advice because they hate my boyfriend so much that I barely talk to them anymore. I got so sick of them lecturing me and now we have drifted apart. You Betches are my last hope. Please help!

Sincerely,
I Should Have Been Named Juliet

Hey Taylor,

Hold on while we turn on "No Scrubs" by TLC. Ugh, there is so much wrong with this situation that if we addressed it all this would turn from an advice column into a multiple page critical essay, so let's tackle why this guy is literally the worst, in list form.

1. He cheated on you.

2. Multiple times.

3. With somebody he was basically having a second relationship with. Is that not the ultimate betrayal? And yet you still call this guy your best friend? How shitty are your friends?

4. You're already making excuses for this guy's shitty behavior. We know love is blind and all, but is it fucking delusional, too? You get cheated on multiple times but everything's all good because "he is young and dumb" . . . K. Quit trying to be "Cool Girl," that shit is not okay and you deserve better.

They say that if all your exes are crazy, the common denominator is you, and here a similar idea applies: If everybody you know hates this guy, the common denominator is probably that he sucks. TBH, he sounds like the textbook definition of a scrub. Like, such a big scrub that the surviving members of TLC met this guy, and then invented a time machine and went back in time so they could write "No Scrubs" about him with Left Eye.

Oh, shit. We didn't answer your question. Talking to your parents, right. We don't think you should tell them about your boyfriend because, really, you should drop him and then it won't matter. Even though your parents sound kinda shallow and even racist, we're not seeing that this guy even treats you right, so it doesn't seem worth the grief telling your parents would cause. If he was an all-around great guy who treated you like a princess and your parents just sucked, sure. But this guy? Not worth the fight.

At the same time, five years is a long fucking time to keep up a con, so we can see why you'd want to clear your conscience (good thing we don't have those). Here's what we think you should do: In the parental dynamic there's usually one parent who's more chill (however slightly) and whom you're closer to—probs your mom. So, one day take her out to froyo or some shit and tell her that you have a problem and you need her help (moms eat that up). Then just break it to her. If your mom's a betch she'll help you think of ways to approach your dad, or she'll just do the work for you. If your parents really are a united front, well shit, it might be time to call a family meeting and break out the PowerPoint.

Good luck. We kinda wanna know how this turns out but if things go south we'd like to maintain some plausible deniability.

You do know how *Romeo and Juliet* ends, right?
The Betches

SPARK NOTES

We know, this chapter was super long. But like, TBH, a relationship is even longer, and if you want to get through it like a betch you should have paid attention. But it's okay, here's the recap, just like "previously on *Mad Men*."

Here's the thing: A guy should *want* to be exclusive with *you* and not the other way around. If you take just any guy on as your boyfriend because he likes you, well, chances are he's not right for you. But we're human (*hot* humans, sure, but humans), and we tend to make a lot of mistakes. But you learn some new shit with each mistake. This means that every good, bad, long, or short relationship you were in taught you something about yourself, hence you are never really wasting your time.

The start of every relationship can be really fun if you do it right. So, don't fuck up and declare you're Instagram official before he even knows you're his girlfriend. Have a lot of sex. Don't say "I love you" first unless you feel super confident that if he doesn't say it back you won't become depressed and Van Gogh your ear off. Make an extremely good impression on his family. Never let him feel like he can do anything he wants, and you won't break up with him. Because you will and then you will get someone else who wants you more. If you fight, don't fly over the Cuckoo's Nest. Say what you want to say, but don't go overboard because, don't forget, you want sweet, sweet make-up sex in the end. That is unless he cheats. Then you're allowed one flesh-wound stab . . . lol half-jk.

7

Commitment and Shit

The "Serious" Relationship, Womp, Womp

Now that you two have been dating for a while you're probably beginning to wonder, could this guy be my future husband? Can I envision spending the rest of my life smelling this dude's morning breath? Can I trust him to never cheat on me? To support me emotionally and probably financially, too? Will his last name look good next to my first name? Is his constant partying something I can learn to deal with, or will I have to pull a Kourtney Kardashian on him and bounce after kid #3?

CHANGING YOUR GUY: ACCEPTANCE VS. CUTTING YOUR LOSSES

At this stage of the relationship, we'll assume you've been dating for over a year. You know your guy pretty well and you're past the honeymoon stage of glossing over all of his weaknesses. His habits are his habits, and if he hasn't changed them by now there's a 99 percent chance he's going to be this way forever. It's at this point that you need to ask yourself: *If this man never changes, will I still love him just the way he is for the rest of my life?*

Answering that question involves being extremely real with yourself and deciphering if the things that really annoy you are things that you can get over or if they'll only make you resent your choice in a few years. What you need in someone at twenty-two is not what you need when you're twenty-eight, and definitely not what you need when you're thirty-four. You have to be able to foresee how your needs will change. Your boyfriend/fiancé/husband should be his strongest self for fulfilling your current needs so that when you're thirty-plus and your ass has dropped three inches and really *need* that thoughtful person, they're there for you.

> *"Men marry women with the hope they will never change. Women marry men with the hope they will change. Invariably they are both disappointed."*
> —Albert Einstein

The hope is that every guy matures with age, but with that logic you wind up as Charlie Sheen's deluded baby mama. Some guys grow up, and other guys stay young and immature forever because they can. The good part about this fact is that it shouldn't matter to you whether your boyfriend is at the height of his maturity or is only going to grow and evolve like the extremely expensive wine you expect him to order at every minor celebration. You should be content with him being at the exact maturity level he is when you decide to marry him, because then you won't be disappointed if he's one of the nonchangers.

Relationships are about a combination of sex, similar interests, and timing. If a guy is not the right person for you at the exact time that you are the right person for him, then it will never work because you both are at different places in your lives. Maybe your guy will be the guy you want him to be in five years but that's a big, fat maybe. Do you want to build a life on a maybe? It's like that barre class you took that morning you were insanely hungover from fifteen tequila shots the previous night. No matter how good your intentions for going were or how bad you wanted a great class, that was never going to be your best class because the timing wasn't right. You'll have to wait for the next class to master your plank.

Likewise, if two people are great together but are at points in their lives where they want different things, it's never going to work. Maybe you're ready to settle down, but he feels like he's too young to get married? Wrong timing. Maybe you're a hot mess and you still crave toxic people, but he is ready for something deeper? Wrong timing. Maybe he wants to move to Boston for a job opportunity but you would literally rather shoot yourself in the face than leave New York. Wrong timing.

Inspirational Fictional Betch: Pocahontas (Disney Version)

Pocahontas was a Native American betch who fell in love with John Smith, a super-white bro whose friend group was not chill with hers at all. Despite having different interests (he was into guns and gold, while she preferred water sports and talking to trees) these two fell in love. Sadly, John got shot and had to go back to England despite having Mel Gibson's almost-American accent. Pocahontas opted to have her own, fulfilling life and stayed behind with her besties. The moral of the story is that two people may really love each other and want their relationship to work out but if the timing is wrong, it might just not be "meant to be." Timing is pivotal and no amount of peace treaties, raccoon sidekicks, or Coachella-inspired face paint can change your relationship if the two of you met at the wrong point in your lives.

HOW DO I KNOW IF MY RELATIONSHIP IS MOVING FORWARD OR DUNZO?

It will be very obvious when your relationship is moving forward because you both will be excited about going on new adventures together (maybe you decide to go to Phuket in a year) and embarking on major milestones (i.e., excuses for housewarming presents) in your life together. You should both be ecstatic at the thought of moving in together, and if engagement is on the table you should obviously be overjoyed at the thought of a legally binding contract securing yourself and your assets to this person for the rest of your life. Cue panic attack for the rest of us, but whatever, you do you.

SHOULD YOU EVER BE THE ONE TO BROACH TOPICS LIKE ENGAGEMENT OR MOVING IN?

If you have a solid relationship, you can talk about anything and you can initiate any conversation you want. If your relationship is strong enough that you're talking about moving in, then you should be able to move in together. Don't demand, but feel free to broach the topic. Ask him where his head is at, etc. Ideally you want men to initiate, but a major way you can know if your relationship is real is by noticing whether or not you can say what you want to say when you want to say it.

Communication cannot be underestimated. If you don't say what's bothering you the minute, or day, it happens, then after a while it'll come spewing out of you like a betch who's overdone it on the vodka sodas. So if your boyfriend says you've been a cold-hearted bitch for the past few weeks (above and beyond the fact that that's your usual personality and like, your period is on its way) then it's probably because of some unspoken thing in your relationship that you're hesitant to bring up but are frustrated about. A betch who doesn't say how she feels will ruminate, and before she knows it, she's screaming at her BF at her cousin's bar mitzvah when someone asks if she ordered the chicken or the fish.

Allure and mystery are much more important for your sex life than for real-life relationships. If he's really into you, he'll want to live with you. He won't be terrified that you even asked. But don't be a psycho about it. One guideline: You shouldn't move in together before at least nine months of dating, and that's obviously if you're out of college and have lived alone or with a roommate for a while. Not living together after two years of dating at twenty-two is different than not living together after two years of dating at thirty. But if you've been dating for more than two years and you consider yourself an adult (probs like, over twenty-six), and neither of you have even talked about a future together, then it's probably time to ask why. We're not saying that you should be naming your babies after two years, but your boyfriend should at least show small signs he sees *something* long term. An example of a sign: He makes a joke like "We're going to need two TVs when we live together, there is no way you will ever get me to watch reruns of *One Tree Hill* with you." (Don't worry, he will.)

And sometimes relationships simply hit a wall. One per-

> "This is never gonna go our way / if I'm gonna have to guess what's on your mind."
> —Mumford & Sons

son or both realize that to stay in the relationship would be settling or that they are unhappy with what the other person provides. This usually happens when the next step seems obvious and/or imminent and one person (or both) seems hesitant. If all your friends who have been together around the same amount of time as you are getting engaged or moving in together, and you and your guy haven't

> *"We were on a break."*
> —Ross Geller (P.S. They were, but he shouldn't have done it.)

even approached the subject, someone is about to go on a break. Heads up, though: The stress that other couples' engagement parties and celebratory Instagram hashtags put on a couple who's on the brink of a breakup is very, very real.

It may hurt at the time, but a breakup earlier rather than later is lucky, because the later on the breakup happens, the more damage it causes and people it hurts. Wouldn't you rather your boyfriend tell you that he doesn't think he can do this forever before you have three kids and a mortgage to deal with? Wouldn't you want the person to whom you devoted years of your life to find happiness if you just don't think he's the one for you? Answering the question about where you see this going is the best thing you can do for yourself and your boyfriend.

What Would Karen Do?

When Karen's boyfriend breaks up with her because he doesn't see a future, Karen locks herself in her room and plays Daniel Bedingfield's "If You're Not the One" on blast and, of course, on repeat. To quote: *"If I'm not made for you then why does my heart tell me that I am?"* Again, don't be Karen.

If you've asked yourself the hard questions and you *do* come to the conclusion that while you love your guy and he's great, you just think you can find someone better, don't be devastated. This wasn't a waste of time. Every relationship you have will help you grow into a better partner and person. You learn something about yourself from every breakup, no matter when it comes, and if you're honest with yourself at the end of it, you'll never make the mistake of dating someone with the qualities you didn't like in him again.

Signs You're Ready to Commit to Him for as Long as You Both Shall Not Be Super Annoying vs. Signs You Should Break Up

Ready to Commit	Break Up
You look forward to seeing him every day even when you're only apart for a few hours.	You look forward to his business trips as a chance to finally do whatever the fuck you want for once.
You can imagine his family being your family and are excited to be part of his.	You're constantly fighting with him about the fact that he lets his mom third-wheel your anniversary dinner.
You feel lucky to have found him and he treats you like he feels lucky to be with you.	You feel annoyed all the time and wish he would just grow up.
You let the small things slide, like the fact that he won't take you to a Katy Perry concert.	You're constantly picking fights with him over the fact that he accidentally deleted *Broad City* from the DVR.
You still surprise each other often and are consistently trying to do and see new things together.	He surprises you by forgetting to flush the toilet, and the only new thing you want to explore with him is separate bedrooms.
You guys talk about your future all the time.	You guys talk about your issues all the time.

Relationships are outlets for self-reflection, not shares in a rapidly plummeting IPO that you suddenly had to sell and suffered a complete loss from. Life is a journey and not a rush to cash out your stocks immediately. Don't settle for someone because, according to Instagram, everyone and their mother is getting engaged. Don't settle because you think you'll die alone. Don't settle. Because you're a betch and you deserve the best.

Netflix and Chill, A Definition by Urban Dictionary:

Going to other peoples' homes and fucking them or doing any other hard-core sexual activity.

If you constantly mentally ask yourself if you're settling then you're most probably settling. So go out there and find the perfect bro for you who also thinks you're the perfect betch for him. It's not supposed to be easy. If it were easy it wouldn't be called a "life partner." It'd be called an "I-enjoy-chilling-with-while-watching-Netflix-and-smoking-weed-for-the-next-few-months partner." If it's hard, then when you finally find the bro you want to put up with for the rest of your life, you'll know you did your due diligence. Advances in medicine will probably enable you to live to be well over one hundred. Do you want to spend 75 percent of that time with a guy you think is just okay because you got bored and anxious about settling down at twenty-five?

SEX: HOW TO STAY DRUNK IN LOVE

The beginning of any relationship is a sexual marathon. You guys can't take your hands off each other. You're drunk in love and you want to surfboard him constantly. You have sex like it's a Piperlime going-out-of-business sale. What girl and her boyfriend don't remember the legendary "day of eight times"? You can expect the magic to last for about four months.

After that, the two of you are still into each other but you've really explored each other's bodies more intensely than Donald reviewed Barack's birth certificate. You know what each other likes, what each other doesn't like, what will make you scream, what will make you freak the fuck out because *No! You did not just try to put your finger in there!* You start having sex less and less because you feel secure that when you wake up that person will be there, peeing with the bathroom door open. The mystery fades, and so does the curiosity.

Suddenly, your boyfriend's idea of foreplay is sticking his hand down your pants without taking his eyes off *The Walking Dead*. But if he thinks he's going to get a betch to put out without any real effort he is seriously mistaken. Your sex life should be more exciting than a Bon Iver concert attended without serious drugs.

In general, it's less about the *amount* of sex you have, and more about the *way* that it happens. It's not a huge issue if you only have sex twice a week, but if he's putting no effort into making it somewhat romantic, it's time for your betchier, more manipulative side to come out. You're not a fucking blow-up doll. He needs to work for it, even if that means faking the enjoyment of foreplay.

There is no time when it's more important to keep the mystery alive than at the point in the relationship when the sex has started to fade. No guy wants surpriseless boning for the rest of his life. It may be tempting to let yourself go or to treat sex like it's as routine as brushing your teeth or yelling at your mom, but control yourself. Resist the urge to wear your granny panties and an oversized Yeezus concert tee to bed. Don't stop waxing or shaving your legs. Definitely never fart in front of him.

> **Ro [*on hearing Mr. Hill is cheating on his wife*]:** I don't get it. Mrs. Hill is pretty. I mean, she's really pretty.
>
> **Gina:** Show me a beautiful woman, I'll show you a man who's tired of fucking her.
> —*Perfect Stranger*

Bodily Realities and When They're Okay:

Farting: Never on purpose. If it happens accidentally, that's okay, just laugh it off and refrain from eye contact for like, five minutes. If you're having a really bad night post-intense-Mexican-dinner, take some Tums and consider sleeping on the couch.

Peeing with the door open: Drunkenly peeing with your friends is natural but don't bring that shit home. Do you love watching your boyfriend pee? Exactly.

Shitting: Turn on the shower for noise cancellation. If you're having a serious problem invest in some Beats.

Sometimes men, simple as they are, get in a routine and forget that you're a fucking princess and should be wooed into bed, and sometimes they get distracted because the Internet is for porn. If he's looking at porn when you're not around, that's fine. It's natural that, if he needs to get off, he should be able to do that if you're away. However, if you live together, and he's jerking off alone—and the same goes for you, if you're sneaking off to masturbate—something is wrong. That's what the other person is there for—to save each other the effort.

You need to work on your sex life as you would any other aspect of your life. It requires time, commitment, money, and a little bit of manipulation. For instance, reminding him of the steamy sex life you had when you were blowing him in the back of a taxi or getting banged against the public bathroom wall.

As with all things in life, people want what's elusive and what they feel they cannot have. If he's feeling complacent, like he can have you at any moment he wants without so much as going down on you, it's time to subtly teach him a lesson. Don't actively withhold sex, just be more conscious of how you act in front of him. Stop changing in front of him matter-of-factly and instead just allow him to see your body in its sexiest, best-groomed state. He should be undressing you slowly each night, not watching you squeeze, hop, and pant yourself into your skinny jeans every morning. If he asks why you're suddenly not casually getting naked in front of him anymore, kindly inform him that if he wants to see you naked he has to seduce you.

The mysterious part of a relationship is what attracted you in the first place. Mix things up, try some toys and/or role-playing. You can still be classy—you don't have to be a black leather, whips and chains dominatrix all the time—but some subtle teasing can keep the mystery alive. If he tries to just jam his hand in your underwear while simultaneously unzipping his own pants, let him know that you're not having sex with him until he kisses you for three minutes. This isn't demanding, it's bossy and it's sexy and that's hot.

The best analogy is: Think about sex the way you think about all the clothes in your closet. Imagine your favorite tops from two years ago. It's not as though you don't like them anymore, it's just that you and everyone else has seen them a million times, so you convince yourself you need new clothes.

> *"Sometimes, I just want to watch* The Daily Show *without him entering me."*
> —Rita, *Bridesmaids*

Just like with sex, you don't NEED to constantly be trying new things, but you WANT to because you fucking refuse to be photographed in those same Rag & Bone jeans one more time. You want new clothes, so you stick those jeans in the back of your closet. But when you find them in two years you're going to be like, *Oh yay now I remember. These jeans look so fucking hot on me.* Bottom line: You are the jeans and your boyfriend is the betch who gets tired of wearing them unless she mixes shit up. As if we needed another excuse to never stop shopping.

A NOTE ON NUDE PICS

Stop. Don't send them. Regardless of how much he badgers or begs. If you absolutely must send them, never, we repeat NEVER, put your face in it. Sure revenge porn has become illegal, but that doesn't mean he won't send your naked pic to all of his friends and his friends' friends. Don't be naive, just because your relationship is all rainbows and rosé now doesn't mean it will definitely end that way. And if it ends very badly, what do you think he's going to do with all those pics of your hot bod? If you think he's going to throw them away then either you're stupid, you broke up because he's a homosexual, or he's like, a good person.

SHOW ME THE MONEY

As we've said, money is a huge fucking issue in relationships. It can make or break things and can often determine the power dynamic within a relationship. Oftentimes betches are confused about money. Like, you're a feminist, so you know you should make equal amounts of money for the same work that men do, but also you don't want to be paying for dinner and shit.

It's biological that women want to be taken care of. Sure you're a *grown woman I do whatever I want,* but there is a certain femininity that comes with letting a guy assemble your dresser or buy you a gorgeous bracelet, and be like, *Baby, it's you, you're the one I love, you're the one I need.* In the days of cavemen, the men would bring home the slain tigers or mammoths or whatever while the women skinned them to make the fur coats. You want a guy with muscles for the same reason you want a guy with money; an innate need for protection for you and your kids. Men are biologically bigger than women and so should feel an intrinsic need to protect their girlfriends physically and financially. It's human nature, and you should let him take care of it. Teamwork is important but like, it's always better when men do the heavy lifting.

The Evolution of Money and Dating

When a man is trying to get your attention (a.k.a. sleep with you) while you are dating, you should let him impress you. The easiest way for him to do that is to buy you shit. That means he should be paying for all of dinners 1 to 3. Again, you should always offer, no one likes someone who automatically assumes she's being comped, just like the way you wouldn't like a guy who automatically assumes he's getting laid on any occasion.

Once you're in a real relationship things become more symbiotic. Unfortunately this means you have to pay for more shit, but fortunately you should never be splitting everything down the middle. "But paying for half of everything is what's fair!" your bra-burning nicegirl cousin will argue. Who gives a shit about fair? We live in an unjust world filled with atrocities and institutional sexism and cold-pressed juice costs $11. Deal with it.

To give you a rule, every eight dates you go on as a couple you should insist on paying for one full meal. Of the remaining seven, the guy should pay for four full dinners and you two should split the last three. Who said you were never going to need to know how to use math after your SATs? Let's break this down into simpler terms. You should be paying something for at least half of your excursions and there are some times, albeit rare, where you should be paying for the whole thing. Paying for a nice dinner for your boyfriend is a power move and shows that if you wanted to, you could pay for a lot of things but you don't, because you deserve to be treated like Kate Middleton. When do you think was the last time that betch pulled out her credit card? On her eighth date with William, that's when.

You may think that a guy being extremely wealthy should void this rule, but it's quite the opposite. Paying for random things shows that you're not just using him for his money. You genuinely enjoy his company, and the fact that he's really rich is just a ~~total necessity~~ nice perk.

On the flip side, if you're in college and you have a boyfriend who doesn't make his own money (which most college-aged guys don't), you should pay for half most of the time because you're both poor as fuck and those Barton shots aren't buying themselves.

All this talk about the men always paying for shit does not mean your relationship is not equal. You simply bring a nonmonetary type of giving to the table. People have different ways of expressing how much they care

> "Someone gave me the Love Languages *book,* and that has been the best book I've ever read about relationships and has helped me the most."
>
> —Kristin Cavallari

about others and have different expectations of how someone should show them they love them. Gary Chapman's *The Five Love Languages* basically says that there're five ways that people show that they care about someone they love: Gifts, quality time, words of affirmation, acts of service, and physical touch.

Most betches appreciate gifts but like, we also like to be told how amazing we are. But if a guy is showing you he loves you by buying you that Chanel bag you've been eyeing for like, forever, you need to reciprocate with something that you know he loves, which usually isn't money unless he's Kanye. Read the handy chart below and then act accordingly.

His "Love Language" (barf)	What You Should Do
Gifts	Surprise him by buying his favorite cologne (which is a gift for you, too, fucking duh).
Quality Time	Skip your girls' dinner to be with him when his dog dies.
Words of Affirmation	Tell him he looks so fucking hot before you guys leave for a party.
Acts of Service	Pick up dinner and walk his dog if he's super busy at work.

His "Love Language" (barf)	What You Should Do
Physical Touch	Play with his hair while you guys watch TV. The occasional not-on-your-period blow job also never hurt anyone.

You should always be giving 50/50 in a relationship, so if you want the thoughtfulness and gifts, maybe he wants the time. If you're going to be draining this guy's bank account, you need to show him you care in other ways that he can't get from anyone else. If you don't, then you're fucking useless—what are you bringing to the table? No one wants to be with someone who spends their money and treats them like shit. Even Britney Spears eventually came around to this fact.

MOVING IN: BOYS? YUCK

After you've been with your boyfriend for a long period of time and like, your lease is up, it's pretty standard to wonder whether or not you want to move in with him. But it's tricky. The moment you move in with your boyfriend is the last moment you will ever really be alone. Which as a confident, independent betch naturally sends you into a fear and anxiety spiral.

Does that mean I can't walk around in my period shorts anymore? Will my armpits always have to be shaved? Will I never be able to fart in the comfort of my own bed? Wait a min-

ute, will I forever have to pretend I'm taking a shower every time I take a shit? What if I have Chipotle!??!?! The fucking horror.

We meannnnnn, yes, all of the above are true. The essence of moving in with someone is losing the freedom of doing whatever you want whenever you want. The goal is to find someone who loves you for you and doesn't resent you for watching *Keeping Up with the Kardashians* marathons all weekend or wearing the same bra for two weeks straight.

When you are contemplating moving in with someone, it reminds you that this is supposed to be forever. The last time you have your own bed. The last time you can reasonably expect him to not see what's under the bathroom sink. Everything will be "ours." Your life will be completely exposed to the person whose opinion you care most about. It's some intimidating shit. But everyone who's ever been married or cohabitated has done it. So either the vast majority of every person who has ever lived has fucking lost it or they did it when they knew the sacrifices were absolutely worth it.

So you've thought about it and decided this guy is worth having to mingle your dirty clothes in one hamper. Here are some guidelines when moving in with your boyfriend:

Rule 1: Do not move into a studio. In the rare case that you are extremely easygoing and don't care about someone constantly being in your space 24/7, this may work for you. Consolidate your clothes and rent storage space. For the rest of us normal people, living in one room with another person—even if that other person is Ryan Gosling—sounds like Hell. When you have a fight, where do you go to calm down? The closet? On a more positive note, if you can survive living in one room with your boyfriend you can probably get through almost anything.

Rule 2: Decorate with him in mind. Every guy thinks he has "style." Unfortunately their style is less "comfortably chic" and more "on sale at Target." As long as you let him install his video game console on the big TV, you're allowed to decorate the apartment to your standards. You can make it girly as long as you don't cramp his "style." Which means you can use your pretty throw pillows, as long as your couch isn't hot pink.

Rule 3: Don't beg for a ring. Just because you live together doesn't mean you are automatically engaged. A guy moves in with a girl to see if it's the right fit. So should you. If you're a mature betch, you will have marriage conversations when you both are ready, not every time *My Best Friend's Wedding* is on TNT. In most cases, moving in is a big enough step for a guy that he needs a little time to process it before getting ready for the next stage. For women, we like to think ahead and think about the future so we get excited about getting engaged, especially when one of our friends does. Don't Emotionally Masturbate your way to the next stage and forget to enjoy the low-pressure "living together" phase. Listen to that poster on your loser coworker's wall and Keep Calm and Carry On, taking every day as it comes. Once you both have had extensive, naturally timed talks about getting married and are obviously on the same page, then the betchiest way to hint at getting engaged without ruining the surprise is to take a screenshot of the exact ring you want with specs and save it on his bathroom iPad. He'll thank you later.

Rule 4: Be coy about your bathroom habits. This is a big one for women. Boys say that girls don't shit or fart, but you don't want to live with a little boy. Your boyfriend, a mature bro, might also say it as a joke, but he obviously knows that betches go to the bathroom. It's a fact of life. Just be coy about it. Go when he's distracted, turn on music or something, leave some spray or candles in the bathroom. Do not, under any circumstances, leave the door wide open. So, if you're good about it and he still says *ew* or *gross* and is serious, remind him your ass doesn't exist for the sole purpose of allowing him to keep alive the hope to one day stick his dick in it. And honestly, no guy will ever be like, *Well we moved in together, but I just couldn't handle her gas.* So keep eating that quinoa, betch, it's good for you.

The moral of the moving-in story is that you never know how much you hate someone until you live with them. You get to see how they handle life from day to day. You begin to learn and gauge what you're willing to put up with and do to make your relationship work. It's really about meshing and putting in equal amounts of effort, and is the start of you two making decisions as a couple. So if his open-door dumps and coaster-less parties are bothering you two months in, this isn't looking good for your future.

ULTIMATUMS: ARE THEY EVER OKAY?

If you ever have to give an ultimatum, it means that you and your boyfriend are not on the same page, which means you are probably on the verge of a breakup. Let's say you're with a bro for six years or so, and you're ready to get married, and when you bring it up you learn that he simply isn't. What do you do? *Will he ever be ready? Did you waste six fucking years on this commitmophobe? Am I really going to be thirty-one and single again? SERENITY NOW!!!*

The truth is, if you give this guy an ultimatum, as in "marry me or it's over," the only way to a future of marital bliss is through breaking up. Because basically, you just threatened him, and if he proposes you'll always know he's just doing it because he's scared of you, not because he wants to wife you up. He will resent you for it. But if you break up, there's a chance he'll realize that he needs you in his life and will come running with a (big) ring. In this scenario, the proposal will be his choice, and it won't result in bitterness. However, if you break up and he doesn't come after you, it's going to be fucking depressing, but you'll have to remember that this bro didn't want to marry you anyway so the more time you stayed together the more and more hard boiled your eggs would have become.

To avoid giving ultimatums, you should discuss with your boyfriend how you both feel about marriage beforehand. Like, *years* beforehand. When you want to get married. How many kids you want to have. Blah blah. Get all the boring shit out of the way in the beginning, so you aren't totally shocked when it matters the most.

Even though *He's Just Not That Into You* is a dumb fucking movie that at first teaches valuable dating lessons, but in the end regresses into a romantic comedy to which pathetic girls can Emotionally Masturbate with a tub of frozen yogurt, it has one redeeming story line: Jen An giving Ben Affleck an ultimatum, to which he says no, so she leaves him. After some time Ben comes after her with a stupid laundry khaki pants (ew) proposal that we would never really go for. Anyway, the point is that he would have never done it if she had stayed with him, and she would never have been that happy if he'd reluctantly agreed to marry her in the first place.

And despite that they both agreed to never get married when they just started dating (yes we're still going on about this movie), we all know Jen An was lying to herself and just thought, *Whatevs, he'll prob change, I'll "just go with it."* (Yes that is also the title of another romantic comedy Jen An happens to be in and irrelevant to this point. Hollywood, stop pigeonholing Jennifer!) The reason, though, why her ultimatum resolved positively is because it's a dumb fucking movie.

Don't expect a guy to change. If, a year into the relationship, he tells you he doesn't want to get married or says that he doesn't believe in monogamy, run as fast as you can. Yeah it's *possible* he doesn't realize he wants to marry you yet and will realize it after five more years together. But it's more probable that time will go on and he'll be comfortable with the fact that you stayed despite his feelings. If you want to get married, your boyfriend should at least have it on his radar for the future. If not, say *bye bitch,* and move on.

Does the Guy Just Know?
by Head Pro

Imagine, if you will, a recently engaged couple. The bride-to-be beams brightly as friends and loved ones clamor for her hand, as though they are the concert crowd and she is Justin Bieber. Meanwhile the groom smiles sheepishly, trying to avoid showing too much emotion while his buddies offer him "wink-wink-nudge-nudge" congratulations, which are frankly pointless in 2016 because by now the couple has had sex more times than they can count.

Then, it happens. One of the girls breaks out of her betrothal fever dream to approach the groom. After some surreptitiously judg-y praise for his choice of ring, you see the look on his face emerge. His bashful smile evolves to a grimace, as if someone had begun to slowly drag his ball bag across a cheese grater. You know that she has just asked the question men everywhere dread: "How did you know she was the one?"

Guys hate this question, because the truth is that, yes, guys do "just know." But most guys hate admitting it, because paradoxically it makes us look like we're hiding something. People want to believe that everything in life (things they want but don't have, specifically) are the result of some "secret" they haven't yet stumbled upon. A fulfilling career. A hot, sexy body. A functional golf swing. And, yes, a blissful relationship.

That's why people probe for more information when guys say, "I dunno, I just did." "Well, how long have you been together?" they ask. "Where did you meet? Where was your first date? *When* did you know?" Something, anything to get him to spill the beans as to how this couple is so happy and the asker is still a lonely loser.

The truth is that there is no secret, no "engagement chicken" you could cook, no cool trick you could do with your tongue that will compel a man to spend the GDP of a small nation on a compressed piece of carbon. We just know. Obviously, compatibility and general happiness play a part. So do the little things: How well do you rebound from fights? Are you fine hanging out doing nothing, in silence? Are you still happy to see her long after the hormonal puppy love has died down? Age and maturity matter, too. A guy can be over the moon for you at twenty-two, but if he's just not ready to get married, he's never popping that question. Change twenty-two to thirty-two for some guys, and the answer remains the same. Everyone's different.

Basically, it'll happen when it happens. Just don't ask him how he knew if you won't be satisfied with "idk" as an answer.

GETTING ENGAGED: TWO SOULS, ONE SHINY ROCK

The best part of the whole getting married thing is definitely getting engaged. A) You get a new amazing, shiny ring to wear with every single outfit. B) You have an excuse to throw several parties. C) You don't have to worry about not getting married someday. D) Soon you're going to have like, a backup bank account. Ugh so fun.

The one downside of getting engaged, however, is that now you like, have to plan a fucking wedding. Which sounds nice in theory and on Pinterest boards, but in reality is like shooting yourself in the face every single day for an entire year.

First comes setting up a registry, which also sounds fun but isn't in real life because you have to plan the gifts so far in advance. Like, all of a sudden you have a ring on your finger and now you're just dying for a salad spinner? You already live with your boyfriend and manage to cut your own chicken every day, but will scream if you don't have the new Michael Aram gold cutlery set? It makes no fucking sense. Honestly, registry would be much simpler if you could register at Chanel, SoulCycle, or Chase QuickPay.

But let's rewind and talk about the actual engagement, a moment betches talk about sometimes (read: when someone else they know gets engaged) and nicegirls have dreamed about since the moment they exited the womb. The single most important thing about an engagement is that you say *yes* because you actually want to marry this person and not out of fear of embarrassing your boyfriend while he's on the ground on one knee. There's not much else to be said here except: Be sure.

The second most important consideration is how he does it. If he's smart, he better fucking ask the advice of your closest friend or confidante, a.k.a. the person who knows your dream engagement scenario. He should also ask her advice about what kind of ring you want. It's critical that this friend knows not to spill her personal opinions into her advice. Like, if you hate a halo setting but she likes it and then your boyfriend proposes with the nastiest halo princess cut you've ever seen, you should just stop speaking to that friend immediately. She deserves a lifetime of unhappiness. Sorry, but it's true. You can re-set a diamond, you can't re-set a friendship.

Well in advance, make sure to tell him which of your friends to ask when he needs anything that requires surprising you. Then prepare that friend for every eventuality. How you want to be asked, how you don't want to be asked, the type of ring you want, the type of ring you definitely, definitely do not want, how much you want your mom involved, and so on. As long as he's not a total fucking moron who thinks all girls like the same type of ring and getting proposed to on an MLB game Jumbotron, you'll probably get what you want.

Shit Crazy Bitches Do: Broadcast Their Thirst

Do not post on Facebook a picture of the ring you want with the status "Future husband, take note." This advice stems from a real person who did this, and it was like, super embarrassing for her. Didn't her mom ever teach her not to be a pretentious materialistic bitch . . . in public?

Even though the whole breakdown of what your ring and engagement says about you is extremely subjective, we'll do it anyway.

You love going to
Pilates and
brunch with your
besties

You are into
aliens or
really like
pears

You summer in
Nantucket

You still
borrow books
from libraries

You're
probs from
Long Island

You're a
boss betch

You've
considered
boiling
Smartwater

In almost all circumstances—except, of course, for the one in which the bro uses all his savings and buys a ring that leaves him homeless—the bigger the diamond, the happier the fiancée. At least this is true for most fiancées we know. So, maybe casually let your boyfriend know that you're willing to wait for him to propose so that he can save up for a bigger rock. Make the argument that it's better for you because you get to stare at this piece of jewelry you are obsessed with your entire life, which in turn will be a reminder of how much you love him. You can also argue that seeing your big gorgeous ring on your finger might also remind you to give him blow jobs more often. Trust us, he won't have a good defense.

WEDDINGS: DEFINING THE BRIDAL BETCH

The minute you get engaged, everyone on your Facebook feed will start talking shit behind your back about your ring or about how it happened. But you don't care about those people. Those people are "friends," a.k.a. people who exist to be jealous of your awesomely curated Instagram life. No, you only care about what your friends—the ones who will be in the wedding and/or will be hearing you bitch about the wedding—think. Which brings us to a very important point about getting married: Be the Bridal Betch, not the Bridal Bitch.

The Bridal Betch	The Bridal Bitch
Talks about her wedding when people ask her about it.	Won't shut the fuck up about which of her top three favorite napkin holders she should pick. #tablescape
Makes sure her fiancé is involved in decision making.	Bitches that her fiancé doesn't give two shits about the embossing on the wedding invites.
Picks a color scheme for bridesmaid dresses and lets them choose the dress style that looks good on their bodies.	Teal chiffon.
Suggests her bridesmaids spend a moderate amount on her bachelorette to go to Miami or Cabo, where they all get tan and the single ones hook up with randos at the club.	Forces her bridesmaids to spend a shit-ton on the bachelorette to Ibiza and join in on a tradition of wearing really ugly mini-penis swag, the origins of which "tradition" no one actually knows.

The Bridal Betch	The Bridal Bitch
Takes fun, cute pics in which everyone looks good at your bridal shower.	Makes the single people take pics with props and arrows that say, "She's with him," "Taken," and "So jealz."
Gets excited about an understated wedding hashtag, one that involves both your last names and allows people to say, "I normally hate wedding hashtags, but this one's cute."	Gags everyone with a wedding hashtag that's an awful pun and makes people want to come up with new hashtags behind her back. Instead of #KatiesFairyTale they change it to #KatieSuckstheBigD.

So, when planning your wedding, remember that just because the next year is all about you, there's a gentle way of getting people on board with that fact. These should be the happiest days of your life. Why spend them being purposefully left out of a group chat full of your friends shit-talking about how you've become an overbearing bridal bitch?

SO ONCE I GET MARRIED DO I GET TO QUIT MY JOB IMMEDIATELY?

Calm down there, Charlotte York. Now the issue of whether to work or not has like, a shit-ton to do with the situation. The short answer is that you should always be doing *something* besides telling the nanny how to raise your kids. You should always have things to talk about that don't involve you redecorating your house with your husband's money or how big of a shit your toddler took that day. No man wants to come home and have dinner with his housekeeper. You should always be relied upon somewhere outside your home. Whether that's being CEO of a major corporation or being a docent at the natural history museum, make sure you have a life of your own that is separate and independent from his and, most important, gives you interesting shit to talk about.

Now, as we said, the guy should still be paying for more than you do. Unless you're one of the 1 percent of females who aren't bothered by financially supporting a guy, seek out someone who makes more money than you. This is way easier to do if you're a waitress than, say, Sheryl Sandberg or us, but that's all the more reason to search for someone who's your equal or better in ambition and drive.

But even though you should be financially supported, that doesn't mean financially dependent. You don't want to be trapped. You should always be working on something, and ideally it should pay you a decent amount of money. Women have come a long way since our grandmas needed to ask our grandpas for money to buy underwear and bobby pins. It's now acceptable and important to be an independent woman. You can be a stay-at-home type of woman in the future, but only because you made money for yourself in your twenties and thirties. Never underestimate the power that comes with having your own money and being like, *Oh I don't need another BMW, but I could totally buy it if I wanted to.*

Maybe you want more than a decent amount of money. Maybe you want a "fuck-you job" (a job in which you make enough money that if your husband is being annoying enough, you can be like, *Fuck you, I'm out* at any point without having to worry about how to pay for your own froyo). A fuck-you job allows you to base your decision to stay in the relationship purely on the whims of your feelings and not on any financial need. Is this a good thing or a bad thing? That leads us to our next question. . . .

PRENUPS: SHOULD I GET ONE OR ARE THEY LIKE, SO LAST SEASON?

Generally speaking, the person who has less money is the person who doesn't want a prenup. For those of you who are stupid, a prenup is a document that you get *before* marriage that says something along the lines of "if we get divorced, you're not entitled to any of my fucking money."[4] The person with more money usually wants a prenup because it can be easier to deal with a plan for a breakup when both people are being rational and the poor one is not beating the shit out of the rich one's car with golf clubs.

People who are against prenups argue that they can make it too easy to give up on a partnership. Marriages are like the stock market or *Keeping Up with*

> "Maybe you have a trust fund. Maybe you'll have a wealthy spouse. But you never know when either one might run out."
>
> —Mary Schmich, "Wear Sunscreen"

---

[4] Verbiage may vary.

the Kardashians: Riddled with good years and years you want to punch your husband in the face on the daily. Having no prenup makes it harder to get divorced, which means you might be more inclined to stick out those shitty years, which might turn into glorious, obsessed-with-each-other-even-though-you're-old-now years. Then again, they might not, and you might wish you had a prenup if you suddenly win the lottery or your great uncle dies and leaves you a shit-ton of money. There's really no way to know, and we definitely can't tell you what to do with your money, so it's your choice if the risk is worth the potential reward, but as business betches who have dark souls, we lean toward the big P.

STAY HOT, IT'LL MAKE EVERYONE HAPPY

You know that awfully cliché phrase that people say and you're just like, *Uugh shut up?*: *Happy Wife, Happy Life!* Yes, it's really annoying, but it's also really true. You know what else is painfully true? As time goes on, shit starts to droop.

One day you look in a mirror and notice a few lines forming around the eyes. Despite four Pilates classes a week, the ass is still jiggling. The veins on the ankles begin to come to the surface. This honestly sounds like a horror movie and that the person we're describing is the monster. But no, that person is you! In like, fifteen to twenty years!

But just because you're slowly turning into the Loch Ness Monster (read: old person) does that mean you can just like, give up on yourself? Does that mean you can order dessert every time you go out to dinner? That you can start shopping at Filene's Basement? Fuck that.

If you do, your husband is not going to want to have sex with you and your marriage will crumble into pieces. Note the distinction, though: We are not saying that he won't want to have sex with you because you're getting fat and ugly. No, he won't want to have sex with you because you are *letting yourself* get fat and ugly. The ugliest you'll ever be is unhappy. Wallowing around in unhappiness is why you're ugly AF.

A confident betch is happy with how she looks. She's happy with whom and what she surrounds herself. She still likes to have sex and generally gives a shit. This is the type of woman you want to be for the rest of your life.

Why? Because taking care of yourself and having a positive outlook attracts people to you, including your husband. The minute you start to give up on yourself is the minute he starts to give up on you.

And *of course* this is absolutely the case for him, too. If he thinks the obese version of the dad bod is cool, well, then he can sleep in the pool house until he gets his fucking fat ass onto a treadmill. At no time in your marriage should your husband think for a second that if you wanted to, you couldn't leave and have dozens of guys trying to date you, whether you're twenty-six or seventy-six. The key to the subtle manipulation of marriage is always letting your husband know that you're a prize that he should be admiring and lucky to have. So what's a betch to do? Two words: Stay hot. Your husband will be happy. You will be happy. You will also still be having orgasms and you'll never have to see what the inside of Filene's Basement looks like because if it's anything like our parents' basements, well, then it's a win-win for you. That shit is from like, *Saw IV*.

No man is going to opt for hair plugs and staying in shape if his wife of twenty years looks as worn out as a 2005 *Us Weekly* at a nail salon. Staying in shape mentally and physically means you still give a shit about where you're headed in life and you still have a lot to offer. Relationships are work and giving up on beauty maintenance is equivalent to giving up on life. Elizabeth Taylor's eighth marriage was at age sixty. She was a power betch who never settled for any guy who didn't make her happy and know she was hot shit. And she was able to have this confidence at age sixty because she made sure she always looked amazing.

How to Avoid the Marriage "Trap" by Head Pro

So you're married! Congratulations, may your life be filled with love, happiness, and dozens of Crate & Barrel gift cards with $3.41 on them that you'll never consolidate. This book obviously isn't as heavy on marriage as it is on the other, earlier aspects of dating, because as smart and talented and good-looking as we are, marriages are all different. One thing I do want to talk about as a guy, though, is the idea of your new hubby feeling "trapped" in your marriage. No, this is not exclusive to men, but you don't look to me for tampon advice, and I don't ask you for help building my fantasy football roster, so let's both stick to what we know, shall we?

What Does It Mean to Feel Trapped?

Obviously, you know what the word itself means, right? I mean if not, there are probably some concepts in this book you've had a hard time with. It means being unable to escape somewhere, which in terms of marriage is obviously metaphorical (unless you're like, *really* crazy). When people read about a guy complaining about feeling "trapped" in his marriage, they usually assume that he's saying he wants to fuck other girls and is regretting his decision to enter into holy matrimony. That's not really it, though. Feeling trapped isn't (just) about sex and, unlike the time you chained your prom date to your radiator for taking a selfie with your best friend, it doesn't necessarily mean he wants out.

Feeling trapped for guys is ultimately about powerlessness, hopelessness, and an inability to effect change and control his own destiny. Part of that is the learning curve inherent to marriage—we come from a culture that values and exalts men who create their own rules and live life on their own terms, and that's a shitload harder to do when you're not the only one who has to look at the ultrasweet Miller Lite neon sign hanging in the living room. But it's also a sign of unmet expectations and unspoken reservations. A man who feels "trapped" in his marriage is one who comes home every day feeling like he's powerless to fix, improve, or move things forward, either from his own perspective or overall. Imagine working at a job you hate: There are things you like about it, sure, and you're not going to leave because you need to work, so instead you show up and just go through the motions, knowing that it won't get any better than this. That's what it's like to feel trapped.

Whose Fault Is It If My Husband Feels Trapped?

Unfortunately, it's not that simple. If you're dating and you decide that you don't like the direction things are going and want to leave, you can just do that. When you're married, though, it's obviously more complicated, and one partner's problem is now both of your problems. But the truth is, more often than not, it's the men who get themselves stuck in these ruts. Society tells men to take charge and be in control, but healthy relationships don't really work that way, and we don't do a great job of making men aware of the tools at their disposal to cope when they aren't sure of how to handle things.

This is all assuming you're not a horrid, horrid bitch, obviously. Like, if you were one person before you got married and then turned into some kind of monster as soon as you said "I do," then that's going to fall pretty squarely on your shoulders. But that's not most people, and hopefully not you. So unless you're two years into your marriage and haven't fucked since your honeymoon because you don't think he's "earned it," it probably has to do with your husband's emotions and not some shortcoming of yours.

How Can We Avoid This?

The bad news is that sometimes the feeling of being trapped is unavoidable. The good news, though, is that's because it typically comes in phases and doesn't ultimately mean much in the end. If you want to do your part to keep things fresh and interesting to minimize these feelings for your manbaby of a husband, consider the following:

Sex: It's pretty common for sexual frequency to drop a bit after a while, and that's not necessarily the end of the world. As long as you're doing it a couple of times per week, you're well within the national average. More important, though, is keeping it interesting. Even the most creative couples run out of ideas, and both parties can begin to feel like the sex is just a matter of going through the motions. Fortunately, the Internet is awash with vibrators, toys, and other sex enhancers (no, not pills) that can make sex more exciting in a hurry. You may want to talk it over with him, but you'd be surprised how open most guys are to that sort of thing. The fact that you're taking interest in actively improving your sex life is exciting in and of itself.

Delegate Responsibilities: In modern times, it's unlikely that you'll fall into the convenient "inside versus outside" divisions of labor—there's not a lot of firewood for him to split when you're living in a one-bedroom apartment. But men enjoy feeling like they have a purpose in a relationship, so it's better to outline some clear responsibilities whenever possible. This is pretty easy—just agree to do the things you hate the least. If you can't boil water and he's allergic to dish soap, there you go. Maybe he feeds and walks the dog in the morning, and you do so when you get home in the afternoon. Most decent men feel pressure to do more around the house, so everyone will be happier if they know their responsibilities.

Go on Dates: This is the most trite marriage advice in the world, but it's popular for a reason. Make time for each other. Go to new places and experience new things. It's decidedly unsexy sounding to schedule romance like that, but it's a lot sexier than having no romance at all. As a plus for your husband, this is a good way to tap into his "pursuer" instincts that he hasn't really needed to flex since the two of you became serious.

Travel Together: One difficulty with marriage is that after a while you kind of learn everything there is to know about each other. Since your husband transforming into a completely different person would be both unlikely and a good reason to call the authorities, you may as well change your surroundings if you can't change each other. Not a lot of people these days have the time or money to take long, exotic vacations, and you don't need to. Visit a nearby city for a long weekend, if that's all you can swing. The point is to experience new things together, as well as the joy that comes with seeing your spouse react to something different than your four walls and questions about the throw pillows.

Communicate: Again, trite for a reason. Look, guys are emotional idiots—we feel things the same way you do, but we're morons when it comes to expressing ourselves in meaningful ways. If you can give us an opportunity to open up, however, that helps. Even simply asking how his day went is all the invitation most guys need to talk about what's bugging them. Communication doesn't have to be formal or awkward, either. All the other things on this list, picking out sex toys and planning cleaning schedules and trips? Those are all opportunities to communicate. It isn't sexy, but marriage rarely is.

In general, people feel trapped in a marriage when they feel like they no longer have an active role to play in it. Love doesn't sustain a marriage; effort, work, and mutual regard and respect for each other do. That doesn't mean it can't be fun, but it does mean that sometimes, you have to think about someone other than yourself for a change.

Dear Head Pro,

My boyfriend and I have been dating for almost a year. He loves me, treats me so well, tells me he wants to be with me long term, etc. Only problem—I want to have sex more than he does. When we have sex, it's great, but it happens a few times a week, when he wants it, whereas I'd be down for sex pretty much any time. Sometimes I initiate, and he's just not in the mood or he's tired, which leaves me sexually frustrated. He's also in his late twenties—I've read libido can slow down for guys around then. I've talked to him about it a few times, and he's said he'll go down on me more/try harder, but not much has changed. I'm not sure how much is fair to ask if he just has a lower libido than me—it's never acceptable to pressure someone into sex.

Like I said, other than this, the relationship is great. So I wanted a pro's opinion—what is considered a "normal" sex drive range for a guy in his late twenties? I know he's making an effort, but why wouldn't he want to try harder to satisfy me? How should I interpret times when he just doesn't want to have sex? Also, when do you think problems with sex can be a dealbreaker for a relationship?

Sincerely,
Not Getting Enough

Dear Not Getting Enough,

Yeesh, what a shitty problem to have. I think to explain it (outside of any medical/psychological terms, since I know nothing of those), let's for a moment divorce the notion of "needs" from "libido," even if in practice that's not that simple. Basically, throughout life you're constantly juggling the most basic needs, like food, sex, shelter, etc. When you're younger, the basic needs are all you really have to worry about—your life just isn't that complicated. In college, things like shelter and food are pretty much covered, so sex gets a lot of attention. I'm not so sure that sex, as in the actual act of it, is really a "need." After all, plenty of, say, Catholic priests take vows of celibacy, and some of them even sustain it without diddling little kids. I think it points more to a general need for intimacy and connection with other people, and when you're young and just figuring things out, sex is an easy way to satisfy that need, especially for a developing brain.

As we get older, like your boyfriend, our needs become both greater in number and more complex. For your boyfriend, those basic things are pretty easy by now. Instead, he's worrying about his career path in a much more nuanced way, planning for his future, and wondering what he's going to achieve in life. Intimacy/sex is still a need, but guess what? He lives with you. So, not only is that another need he has under control, but in your evolved relationship he's fulfilling his need for intimacy in ways that are more meaningful than just having a fuck buddy could ever be. Basically, he doesn't "need" sex as much because he has something better. He may have always had a weaker libido than you, and now that you're closer, it's more obvious because he's having his needs met in other ways.

Knowing that doesn't really help you much, but I think the key is to approach it on those terms. Instead of "pressuring" him, find a way to let him know that sex is something you need not only in and of itself, but also as a way to bond and as an expression of intimacy. Make it deeper than "you're not fucking me enough."

It's also worth noting that for married couples (I know you're not, but still), 2 to 3 times per week is actually dead-on average, so don't think of his libido in a vacuum—you are a couple, after all. If you want more, you might just have to take more, at least until more frequent sex becomes part of your routine and he gets the idea. Pay attention to when he's more receptive to it, and go for it.

I think frequency of sex would have to be at one extreme or the other for it to be a dealbreaker, but in your case, what's more concerning is that it always seems to be about him. If you express yourself and continue to take the initiative and he still doesn't start to reciprocate, at some point he's just being inconsiderate, and that's when you'll have a decision to make.

Infrequent Kisses,
Head Pro

SPARK NOTES

Can you believe this book is almost done? We know, we'll miss you, too. Here's what just happened in this chapter in case you missed something.

You've made it to the long-term relationship with your boyfriend, which means you two are in it for the long haul. *So, can I stop caring now?* you might ask but we say *No bitch!* You have to work at a relationship for like, ever. Yeah it's annoying, but it beats being a spinster at fifty-five.

Before you totally decide to settle down with your guy you have to remember you can't secretly hope that he's going to change someday. You need to accept him the way he is now so you have no expectations, which are only going to end in disappointment. However, if he does change (for better or for worse) it will be something you deal with together rather than something forced upon or by you.

You should always be moving forward and honest throughout your relationship. This includes being open with your feelings at all times. The only area to keep it enigmatic is your sex life. Not only does this mean keep him wanting it, but also it's extremely important to be demure with your farts and bowel movements. For everyone's sake.

Don't rush all of the milestones. Moving in, getting engaged, and being married don't need to happen within a year of each other just because you can't wait to throw a big party. Because once you're married like, then what? Kids? Fuck that. They're loud, and you'll never take a vacay to Cabo without having to pay for a nanny again. Make sure you are both ready for each step.

Once you are married, happy, and still hot, do everything in your power to keep yourself happy outside of your relationship. This means working hard, going out with your friends, and looking after yourself. It's kind of like being happy and confident in order to find a guy. Now you have to be happy and confident in order to keep him. Comes full circle, doesn't it? We know, we're like, really smart.

Conclusion

You Can *Still* Skip This Part

Hey Betch, you can pop that bottle of rosé right now, if you haven't already drunk three, because you now know everything there is to know about dating and relationships (or at least, everything that we felt like talking about). If you're blind and had trouble reading this book, you're in luck. Get someone who can read this aloud to you because we're now about to break down this book's important facts, opinions, and hilarious commentary.

Before you can even embark on U.S.S. *Deal with a Guy's Shit Forever*, otherwise known as a relationship (lol double naval pun), you have to like yourself first. This is a lot harder than it sounds because it means not beating yourself up every time you look at your problem areas in the mirror or not feeling too shy to speak up in a group conversation because you don't think you're funny or smart enough or whatever. This means being *really* over your ex-whatever. This means walking down the street, in clothes you love, and feeling legitimately fierce AF. The moment you truly love yourself both mentally and physically is when you develop real confidence, which is one of the most important traits to have in order to start dating. If you don't love you, then why should a bro love you?

How to date: 1) look pretty 2) feel pretty 3) say what you mean 4) hold back in your actions. Even though it's last, number four is perhaps most essential to the dating process. You may want to text a guy you've been on two dates with like, eight of your twenty feelings but one feeling will suffice, if even that. This analogy can apply to almost everything you do at the start of a relationship. You really want to have sex with a guy, and you'll prob end up giving him a blow job, but just hard-core making out and maybe a little groping would suffice. Holding back makes guys want you more. It's science, betches.

> "We accept the love we think we deserve."
> —The Perks of Being a Wallflower

Ever heard of Emotional Masturbation? No? Well, that's because we made it up. That is, we gave a name to a very real epidemic in the female population. Emotional Masturbation means spending the rest of your week daydreaming about the wedding of you and the guy who said "yo" to you in an UberPool. EM is really bad for you because you can become attached to a dream version of someone who is probably a boring asshole. In short, don't put the penis on the pedestal.

Sex: Don't be a prude. Sex is fun. If you don't have it, then your boyfriend is just a friend, right? It also makes you happier, relieves tension, and is exercise. If he stops giving a shit because of the routine or some other issue in your relationship, then take away some of his intimate privileges. *Like, no you can't shower with me if you don't go down on me. K Bye.* Mix shit up, be vocal, be bold. And if he's still indifferent or difficult, kindly remind him that if he doesn't want to do it, someone else will.

> *"I'm not a stop along the way. I'm a destination."*
> —Blair Waldorf

The most important thing to remember in any relationship, be it with yourself or with a guy, is that you should always do your best. Yes, that obviously means you should be caring and give a shit about your significant other, but what's also extremely important (and that no one talks about) is the significance of not letting yourself go. If you're a middle-aged divorcée no one's going to care that you were a knockout when you were twenty-five. You need to make sure you're always looking your best because then you'll not only look great, you'll feel great and most of all, your husband will still want to fuck you.

Sex is key to any long-term relationship, so don't think just because you got a ring you can relinquish any mystery you have. Keep your Botox discreet, make sure you hit the gym, and keep doing things that make you interesting, like taking classes or volunteering. This will make you happier and your relationship stronger and it will also make your husband try harder so you don't wake up one morning next to Brendan Fraser. Don't be the miserable fat housewife with no way out. Always look and feel your best.

> *"You must not know 'bout me/I could have another you in a minute."*
> —Beyoncé, "Irreplaceable"

All of the advice you got in this book is based on our life experiences and the stories of us, our friends, families, enemies, and celebrities. Take all of this shit with a grain of salt because honestly, we made a lot of it up. There are obviously a lot of exceptions to the rules we lay out in this book. There are seven billion people in the world, at least like, five of them will marry a person they fuck on the first date. Having said that, this book is mostly comprised of hard truths that will work for you 95 percent of the time. Did we also just make up that statistic? Yeah we did, whatever. Get used to it.

If you're happy doing what you're doing and after reading this, you slam it down while texting your bestie that we don't know shit about shit and he's like, totally going to text, that's totally fine. We've been delusional before, too. We know it takes many years of life experience and many comforting bottles of Malbec to realize that not everyone will love you.

This book is meant to help identify those assholes before they waste any more of your time.

We've been through it all. We've dated nice guys, mean guys, commitmophobes. Bros with daddy issues, bros with mommy issues, bros with drug issues, intimacy issues, and no issues. We've read dating books, studied psychology, talked to assholes, talked to our friends (some of whom are assholes), talked to happy people, talked to miserable people, and talked to people who have no idea what the fuck they're talking about all in an effort to bring you this masterpiece.

> *"You know how advice is. You only want it if it agrees with what you wanted to do anyway."*
> —John Steinbeck

One thing we have learned is that there are three things that are certain in life: Death, taxes, and the importance of having game. Sure times change, technology has made dating easier yet simultaneously more complex, and social media increased the need for strategy and manipulation. But romance, staying desired, and keeping a guy always wanting more will always be true whether it's 1916 or 2016. So rip the tags off that crop top, pour a vodka soda, and go have yourself anything but a "nice" time. It's fucking Saturday night.

Acknowledgments

We'd like to take a break from thinking about ourselves to acknowledge the people that helped us write this book and pushed us to become the semi-mature young adults that have written our second masterpiece.

To Alyssa, for "showing us the money," pushing us to not be lazy even when we really, really wanted to be, and believing in our ability to work moderately hard when we put our minds to it. To Kate, for still being our favorite nicegirl and whose comma placement edits remind us that there's more to books than being really, really ridiculously ~~good looking~~ funny.

We'd like to thank our parents and our siblings for always supporting us in an effort to mold us into the Head Business Betches they always knew we could be, for indulging our insane ideas, and for assisting us in our journey to make a living off of talking about iced coffee, drugs, and dysfunctional relationships.

To our friends, hookups, and boyfriends, whose hilarious

and interesting stories we have listened to, cried over, and then exploited for our own financial gain. Without you guys we would have no content. Therefore, this book is dedicated to you for all that you've taught us about life, friendship, love, and wedding hashtags.

To the Head Pro, whose writing was a pivotal part of this book and whose wit and journalism never ceases to entertain both us and our fans.

We'd like to thank the rest of the Betches team. This includes our staff, writers, interns, our legal team, publicists, developers, sales team, and everyone else who helps us function semi-optimally on a daily basis so we can enjoy the occasional midday nap. And of course, to Sy, for teaching us what taxes are and how to not get investigated by the IRS—yet.

And finally, to our fans and followers who have kept us in business and who learn and laugh with us every day, allowing us to have the greatest jobs in the world. If we weren't as fucked up as you are we wouldn't be able to relate to you in our writing, fashion, and memes on a daily basis, and for that we are eternally grateful.